17/12/'88

To Robin,

love always

Douglas Hyde

LOVE SONGS OF CONNACHT

OTHER HYDE TITLES CURRENTLY IN PRINT
AT IRISH ACADEMIC PRESS

1 *The Songs of Connacht I-III: Songs of O'Carolan, Songs Praising Women, and Drinking Songs,* edited, with an introduction by Breandán Ó Conaire

2 *Language, Lore and Lyrics: Essays and Lectures,* edited, with a preface and introduction, by Breandán Ó Conaire

3 *The Stone of Irish & Other Irish Folktales* (selected from *Legends of Saints and Sinners*)

and a biography by Dominic Daly

4 *The Young Douglas Hyde*

DOUGLAS HYDE LLD MRIA
An Chraoibhín Aoibhinn

Abhráin Grádh Chúige Connacht

LOVE SONGS OF CONNACHT

being the fourth chapter of

THE SONGS OF CONNACHT

Introduction by

MÍCHEÁL Ó hAODHA

IRISH ACADEMIC PRESS

First edition London and Dublin 1893

Reprinted with an introduction by
Mícheál Ó hAodha 1968, 1987

This IAP reprint is a photolithographic facsimile of the first edition and is unabridged even to the extent of retaining the original printer's imprint.

ISBN 0-7165-0029-9

This edition
Printed in Great Britain by
Antony Rowe Ltd, Chippenham, Wilts.

PRINTED IN THE REPUBLIC OF IRELAND AT SHANNON
BY ROBERT HOGG PRINTER TO IRISH UNIVERSITY PRESS

INTRODUCTION

The publication in book form of Douglas Hyde's *Abhráin Grádh Chúige Connacht or Love Songs of Connacht*, in 1893, marked a turning-point in the Irish Literary Revival and revealed a new source for the development of a distinctive Irish mode in verse and poetic prose.

That a steady flow of poetry and poetic dialogue should have its fountain-head in a bilingual publication of mainly anonymous lyrics may prove puzzling to those unaware of the many tributary streams which swell the main current of modern Irish literature.

Just as some thirteen years earlier Standish O'Grady, in his *History of Ireland* dealing with the early sagas and bardic writings, undertook 'the reconstruction by imaginative processes of the life led by our ancestors in this country', Douglas Hyde discovered in the folk-poetry of Connacht a rich deposit of literary ore which was largely unknown to earlier writers and scholars.

Under the title 'Old Gaelic Love Songs', W B Yeats reviewed this book in the October 1893, number of *The Bookman:*

'Dr Hyde's volume of translations *Love Songs of Connacht* (T Fisher Unwin) is one of those rare books in which art and life are so completely blended that praise or blame become well nigh impossible . . .

'The men and women who made these love songs were hardly in any sense conscious artists; but merely people very desperately in love who put their hopes and fears into simple and musical words, or went over and over for their own pleasure the deeds of kindness or the good looks of their sweetheart.'

Yeats praised the linking commentary with which Hyde pieced together the songs and variant verses describing them as 'almost as much a fragment of life as the poems themselves'. Knowing no Irish and writing for readers who like himself could only sample the flavour of the originals in translation, Yeats pays due tribute

not only to the prose versions but to the parallel translations in verse.

On 'If I were to go West', Yeats comments: 'The whole thing is one of "those thrusts of power" which Flaubert has declared to go beyond the reach of conscious art.'

'My Love, Oh, She is my Love' is described as being 'in the curious metre of the original, without being exactly a good English (sic) poem.' He adds, however, that this translation is 'very much better than the bulk of Walsh's and beyond all measure better than any of Mangan's in *The Munster Poets.*'

Eleven years later in a preface to the limited edition of *The Love Songs of Connacht*, published by Dun Emer Press, Yeats wrote more critically of Hyde's achievement:

'This little book . . . was the first book that made known to readers that had no Irish, the poetry of Irish country people. There have been other translators but they had a formal eighteenth century style, that took what Dr Hyde would call "the sap and pleasure" out of simple thought and emotion. Their horses were always steeds and their cows kine, and their rhythms had the formal monotony or the oratorical energy of that middle class literature that comes more out of will and reason than out of imagination and sympathy. Dr Hyde's prose translations printed at the end of this book are I think even better than his verse ones; but even he cannot always escape from the influence of his predecessors when he rhymes in English. His imagination is indeed at its best only when he writes in Irish, or in that beautiful English of the country people who remember too much Irish to talk like a newspaper, and I commend his prose comments to all who can delight in fine prose.'

These Connacht songs had not only a beneficial influence on Hyde's original verse in Irish but on the poetry in Irish of Pádraic Mac Piarais and others. Hyde's discovery of the uses of vernacular Irish in narrative has been either underestimated or ignored. His influence on An tAthair Peadar Ó Laoghaire, who is generally regarded as the first advocate of *Caint na nDaoine* (the vernacular of the Gaeltacht) deserves closer study.

Dr Hyde's double achievement is all the more remarkable when one realizes that his primary aim was not to provide literature in Irish or in an Irish/English dialect but to save the Irish language from death. This ambition, in the later years of his life, did not lend itself to writing in English except for propagandist purposes. He practically ceased to translate into English as a literary pursuit, having set himself the more difficult task of reviving Irish as a spoken cultural language.

Important, however, as is this aspect of Hyde's work for the development of literature in the Irish language, *The Love Songs* have a further significance for the student of modern literature and drama in Ireland. Here can be found the source of what has come to be regarded as the most notable and distinctive characteristic of modern Irish drama – the quality of the writing which gave dialect and English as it is spoken in Ireland a new status in world drama. Hyde in his prose translations not only revealed what Yeats described as 'that beautiful English of the country people who remember too much Irish to talk like a newspaper' but demonstrated its potential as a basis for a new literary idiom of power and flexibility.

Lady Gregory, Padraic Colum and George Fitzmaurice were among the early writers who followed Hyde's example, but this pioneer work reached its apex in the work of John Millington Synge. Some of the most famous passages of poetic dialogue in *The Playboy of the Western World* have parallels in Hyde's versions of *The Love Songs*.

HYDE	SYNGE
I had rather be beside her on a couch kissing her ever than be sitting in heaven in the chair of the Trinity. (Una Bhán)	And I squeezing kisses on your puckered lips, till I'd feel a kind of pity for the Lord God is all ages sitting lonesome in His Golden Chair. (The Playboy)
If you were to see the star of knowledge and she coming in	

the mouth of the road. (Courteous Breed)

And I thought after that you were a lamp from God, or that you were the star of knowledge going before me and after me. (Ringleted Youth)

Amn't I ever seeing the love-light of the star of knowledge shining from her brow. (The Playboy)

Many other examples of casual words and phrases could be quoted but it might be misleading to list examples as Synge knew Irish quite well and must have heard many of these expressions and phrases on his visits to Aran and the West.

Synge was clearly conscious of Hyde's pioneer work for in a review in *The Speaker*, in 1902, of Lady Gregory's *Cúchulain of Muirthemne* he took Yeats to task for stating in the preface that Lady Gregory was the first to use country dialect in a literary fashion pointing out that Hyde had done so much earlier in *The Love Songs.*

That perceptive critic, Ernest Boyd, in *Ireland's Literary Renaissance* concludes as follows:

'*The Love Songs of Connacht* were the constant study of the author of *The Playboy*, whose plays testify, more than any other writer, to the influence of Hyde's prose. In thus stimulating the dramatist who was to leave so deep a mark upon the form of the Irish Theatre, Douglas Hyde must be counted an important force in the evolution of our national drama. Without injustice to the labours of W B Yeats, it may be said that the success of his efforts would not have been completed but for Synge. Had it not been for Hyde, the latter's most striking achievements might never have been known.'

But the last word must be left with Yeats who was not only a great poet but a seer, a man of vision. He concluded his Bookman review of *The Love Songs of Connacht* in the year of publication with a passage which is remarkable not only for its insight but for its sense of loss.

'As for me, I close the book with much sadness. These poor peasants lived in a beautiful but somewhat inhospitable world, where little has changed since Adam delved and Eve span. Everything was so old that it was steeped in the heart, and every powerful emotion found at once noble types and symbols for its expression. But we we live in a world of whirling change where nothing becomes old and sacred, and our powerful emotions unless we be highly trained artists express themselves in vulgar types and symbols. . . . Yes, perhaps, this very stubborn uncomeliness of life, divorced from hill and field, has made us feel the beauty of these songs in a way the people who made them did not, despite their proverbs:

> "A tune is more lasting than the song of the birds,
> A word is more lasting than the riches of the world".

We stand outside the wall of Eden and hear the trees talking together within and their talk is sweet in our ears.'

BIBLIOGRAPHICAL NOTES

Bibliographers and students will be interested in the first printings of some of these songs in newspapers and periodicals prior to the publication in book form. In an article in *The Dublin Magazine* for October-December 1938, entitled 'From the Little Branch to the New Island', Horace Reynolds points out that the earliest versions of any of *The Love Songs* were published in America.

The first to appear was the well-known *The Brow of Nefin* in *The Boston Pilot* on September 1889. In February of 1890 some more songs were published in *The Providence Journal.*

Later in the same year, 1890, *The Songs of Connacht* were serialized in Dublin in *The Nation* and, after its demise, in *The Weekly Freeman*. There were seven chapters in all entitled 'Carolan and his Contemporaries', 'Songs in Praise of Women', 'Drinking Songs', 'Love Songs', 'Songs Ascribed to Raftery' and two chapters of 'Religious Songs'. Only chapters four and seven were published in book form.

Abhráin Grádh Chúige Connacht or Love Songs of Connacht (*Being the Fourth Chapter of the 'Songs of Connacht'*) was first published in book form, in 1893, By T Fisher Unwin, London, and Gill & Son, Dublin. The text was in Irish with an English translation on opposite pages.

This edition was reprinted later and some of these issues were incorrectly described as 'editions'.

In 1904, The Dun Emer Press published a limited edition of 300 copies of *The Love Songs of Connacht*, with a Preface by W B Yeats, which contains the English translations only.

In 1931, Oifig Diolta Foillseacháin Rialtais published the text in Irish of the First Edition but with nineteen poems added which did not appear previously in book form.

In 1922, Martin Lester published *Amhráin Chúige Chonnacht: An Leath-Rann*, which is an expansion of a lecture delivered by Dr Hyde to his students at University College, Dublin. This bilingual work deals with the 'leath-rann' (proverbs and couplets) and does not include complete songs or poems.

The reprint which follows is a facsimile of the 1893 edition.

Mícheál Ó hAodha

August 1968

abhráin grádh chúige connacht

OR

LOVE SONGS OF CONNACHT

(BEING THE FOURTH CHAPTER OF THE "SONGS OF CONNACHT"), NOW FOR THE FIRST TIME COLLECTED, EDITED, AND TRANSLATED

BY

DOUGLAS HYDE, LL.D., M.R.I.A.

(an chraoiḃín aoiḃinn).

PRESIDENT OF THE IRISH NATIONAL LITERARY SOCIETY, MEMBER OF THE COUNCIL OF THE GAELIC UNION. AUTHOR OF "LEABHAR SGEULUIGHEACHTA;" "BESIDE THE FIRE," ETC.

baile-aṫ-cliaṫ.

clóḃuailte le Gill, Sráid Ui Ċonaill.

LONDON: T. FISHER UNWIN. DUBLIN: GILL & SON.

1893.

Τῇ Ἀφροδίτῃ πόλλ᾽ ἔνεστι ποικίλα,
Τέρπει τε γὰρ μάλιστα καὶ λυπεῖ βροτούς,
Τύχοιμι δ᾽ αὐτῆς ἡνίκ᾽ ἐστὶν εὐμενής.

EURIPIDES.

An lá nać ḃféudaim
Bean do ḃréugaḋ
Ní'l an báire liom.

BÁRD ÉIGIN.

Τίς δὲ βίος τί δὲ τερπνὸν ἄτερ χρυσέης Ἀφροδίτης,
Τεθναίην ὅτε μοι μηκέτι ταῦτα μέλοι.

MIMNERMUS.

FUAGRADH.

A Cháirde,

Ní'l ann san leabhairín seo acht aon chaibidil amháin de'n leabhar mór atá mé ag cur le chéile ar "Abhránaibh Chúige Connacht." Tá caibidil le bheith agam ann ar abhránaibh Uí Chearbhalláin nach raibh ariamh i gcló, caibidil eile ar Mhac Cába agus ar Chom-aimsireachaibh an Chearbhallánaigh, caibidil eile ar abhránaibh óil, caibidil ar chaointib agus ar abhránaibh bróin, caibidil ar dhántaibh Mhic Shuibhne agus an Bhaireudaigh, caibidil ar dhántaibh an Reachtaire, caibidil ar abhránaibh eugsamhla, agus b'éidir tuilleadh. Agus i n-éinfheacht leis sin ta mé ag cur rómham cúntas iomlán do thabhairt ar bhárdaigheacht agus ar rannaigheacht na h-Eireann, le somplachaibh ar níos mo 'ná leith-cheud de na miosúraibh no módhaibh-rannaigheachta do bhi aca, i nGaedheilg.

Acht mar atá clóbhualadh na Gaédheilge an-chostasach, agus mar cailltear mórán airgid le gach leabhar, d'iarrfainn ar gach uile dhuine léigheas an leabhar so agus ata sásta leis an gcaoi ann a bhfuil sé deunta—agus go deimhin do rinneas mo dhithchioll leis—líne do chur chugam-sa go tigh Gill, Sráid Uí Chonaill, Baile-ath-cliath, le rádh an nglacfaidh sé na coda eile nuair tiucfaidh siad amach, no an d-tiubhraidh sé aon chongnamh dham leis na leabhracha so do sgapadh i n-aisge gan luach ameasg na sgol ann a bhfhuil an Ghaedheilg d'á múnadh anois i n-Eirinn, mar do sgap an duine-uasal an Cliabharach mo "Leabhar Sgeuluigheachta," agus a "Dhuanaire" féin, agus mar do sgap mé féin mo "Chois na Teineadh,"—rud do rinne, mar cluinim, mórán leis na teanga do chongbháil suas ann sna h-áiteachaibh sin. Do thug mo charad agus mo chomh-Chonnachtach féin an t-Athair Mártain Labhrás O Murchadh ó Springfield, Ohio, U.S.A., fiche púnt dam, mar chongnamh ann san gcúis mhaith seó, agus is mian liom m'fhíor-bhuidheachas do chur i n-úmhail dó ann so.

Go raibh buaidh agus beannacht ar mhuinntir na Gaedheilge! agus go saoraidh Dia Éire!

An CHRAOIBHIN AOIBHINN.

Oibreaċa eile leis an g-Craoiḃín Aoiḃinn.

Other Works by the same Author:

"Leaḃar Sgeuluiġeaċta."

viii—261 *pp.*, 8*vo.* *Price* 5/-. *Gill & Son, O'Connell Street, Dublin.*

Containing some sixteen Folk Tales, Riddles, Ranns, &c., in Irish, with copious Notes on the Pronunciation, Vocabulary, and Dialect.

"The multitude of characteristic idioms and of those charmingly expressive turns of speech which one meets with daily among the peasantry is so great as to make the work a perfect treasure-house of rich jewels of thought. . . . Dr. Hyde deserves well, not only of his country, but of all scientific investigators and philologists."—*Freeman's Journal.*

"This is the most noteworthy addition that has been made for nearly a century to modern Gaelic literature."—*Chicago Citizen.*

"His collection of Irish Gaelic Folk Stories is the fruit of years of pious work. He has travelled into every corner of Ireland where the old tongue still lingers, gathering from the mouths of the Irish-speaking peasants the olden stories that linger among them."—*Nation.*

"BESIDE THE FIRE."

lviii—204 *pp., large* 8*vo.* *Price* 7/6. *David Nutt, Strand, London.*

Containing Folk Tales and Fairy Stories in Irish and English, collected from the mouths of the peasantry. With Introduction and Notes, and additional Notes by Alfred Nutt.

"Any reader conversant with the subject will at once recognize the fact that this book is distinctly the most valuable contribution that has ever been made to Irish Folk-Lore. It would be hardly an exaggeration to say that it is the only work in that particular department that is trustworthy in its details and scientific in its treatment."—*Nature.*

"We may say that Dr. Hyde's is the first [collection of Irish Folk-Lore] which has been presented in a form entirely satisfactory to the scientific folk-lorist. . . . Few men know the living Gaelic tongue so well as Dr. Hyde, and he has made it his object to give these fragments of Gaelic tradition exactly as he gathered them from the lips of the peasantry, and with all the collateral information that the scientific investigator can require. The result is certainly one of the most interesting and entertaining books of Folk-Lore that it has ever been our good fortune to come across."—*The Speaker.*

"Perhaps the most interesting part of Dr. Hyde's collection of Irish tales, 'Beside the Fire,' is his Introduction."—*Saturday Review.*

"We trust that his warning, though late, is not given in vain, and that a whole literature will not be allowed to die or to become a fossil in the studies of the Dryasdusts."—*Daily News leading article.*

"Cois na Teineaḋ."

60 *pp., large* 8*vo.* *Price* 1/6. *Gill & Son, O'Connell Street, Dublin*

Containing six Folk Stories in Irish, reprinted from the last volume. With additional Notes, &c.

PREFACE.

My dear Dr. Sigerson,

Allow me to offer you this slight attempt on my part to do for Connacht what you yourself and the late John O'Daly, following in the footsteps of Edward Walsh, to some extent accomplished for Munster, more than thirty years ago. Since that attempt of yours, down to the present day, scarcely an effort has been made to preserve what you then felt to be one of the most valuable heritages of the Irish race—its Folk Songs. I have, in the following little volume, collected a few of these, the Love-Songs of a single province merely, which I either took down in each county of Connacht from the lips of the Irish-speaking peasantry—a class which is disappearing with most alarming rapidity—or extracted from MSS. in my own possession, or from some lent to me, made by different scribes during this century, or which I came upon while examining the piles of modern manuscript Gaelic literature that have found their last resting-place on the shelves of the Royal Irish Academy. The little work of mine, of which this is the fourth chapter—the preceding three having been printed in the now extinct *Nation*—was originally all written in Irish, but the exigencies of publication in a weekly newspaper necessitated the translation of it into English. This I do not now wholly regret; for the literal translation of these songs will, I hope, be of some advantage to that at present increasing class of Irishmen who take a just pride in their native language, and to those foreigners who, great philologists and etymologists as they are, find themselves hampered in their pursuits through their unavoidable ignorance of the modern Irish idiom, an idiom which can only be correctly interpreted by native speakers, who are, alas! becoming fewer and fewer every day. It has also given me the opportunity of throwing some of these songs into English verse—such as it is—in doing which I have differed somewhat from yourself, Mangan, Ferguson, and other translators, in endeavouring to reproduce the vowel-rhymes as well as the exact metres of the original poems. This may give English readers, if the book ever fall into the hands of

any such, some idea of the more ordinary and less intricate metres of the people, and of the system of Irish interlineal rhyming, though I fear that the unaccustomed ear will miss most of it. My English prose translation only aims at being literal, and has courageously, though no doubt ruggedly, reproduced the Irish idioms of the original.

I have, as you will see, carefully abstained from trenching upon anything ever before published, my object merely being to preserve what was in danger of speedy extinction. It is, however, more than time that the best of those gems of lyric song, published by Hardiman, over sixty years ago, in two expensive and now rare volumes, were given to the public in a cheap and accessible form. It is to them the student should first look for the very highest expression of the lyric genius of our race.

I have compiled this selection out of many hundreds of songs of the same kind which I have either heard or read, for, indeed, the productiveness of the Irish Muse, as long as we spoke Irish, was unbounded. It is needless to say that I have taken no liberties with my originals, and, though I have inserted conjectural emendations of many passages and words which to me appeared unintelligible, I have, of course, in every case honestly preserved in foot-notes the reading of the original MSS., or the words of the *vivâ-voce* reciter, no matter how corrupt they may have appeared, and I have spared no trouble in collating manuscripts wherever I could, so as to give the best text possible.

In conclusion, I beg of you to accept this little díoscán, not for its intrinsic worth, if it has any, but as a slight token of gratitude from one who has derived the greatest pleasure from your own early and patriotic labours in the same direction, for, as the poet says:—

'S í an teanga Ġaoiḋeilge is greannta cló,
Go blasta léiġtear í mar ċeól,
'S í ċanas briaṫra binn-ġuṫ beóil.
'S is fíor gur mór a h-áille.

Is mé, le meas mór,

An Chraoibhín Aoibhinn.

TABLE OF CONTENTS.

The poems translated into English verse are here marked with a (†); only prose translations of the others are given.

Abhráin Grádh Chúige Connacht

OR

LOVE SONGS OF CONNACHT

AN CEATRAṀAḊ CAIBIDIL

ABHRÁIN GRÁḊ.

Tar éis na h-abráin-óil fiaḋáine mí-ċúramaċa spórtaċa aéraċa so do léuġaḋ, is ceart caibidil ċontrárḋa ḋóiḃ air faḋ do ḃeiṫ 'gá leanaṁaint. Ní mí-ċúramaċ agus eudtrom aṁáin atá an nadúir Ġaoḋalaċ. Bíonn mar an g-ceudna, inntinn ḃoḃrónaċ faoi an ngreann is áirde, agus má leigeann siad orra ḃeiṫ gan suim i rud air biṫ aċt i spórt agus i bpléráca, ní 'l ann aċt leigean orra. An fear ceudna ḃéiḋeas ag rincge agus ag spórt, ag ól agus ag glaoḋaċ anḋiú béiḋ sé ag maċtnaṁ amáraċ go tinn trom tuirseaċ ann a ḃoṫáinín boċt aonránaċ leis féin ag deunaṁ crónáin air ḃóṫċar imṫiġṫe, air ṡaoġal caillte, air ḃíoṁaoineas an tsaoġail seó, agus air teaċt an ḃáis. Ag sin duit an nádúir Ġaoḋalaċ; agus an duine sin do smuainfeaḋ naċ iad an cineál ceudna de ḋaoinib do rinne na h-abráin árd-ġlóraċa spórtaṁla is-cuma-liom-an-diaḃalaċa sin do léiġeamar ann san g-caibidil ḋeireannaiġ, agus do rinne na dánta fíor-ċaoine míne maiseaċa gráḋaṁla ḟeicfeas sé ann san g-cuid seó i láṫair, tá sé go mór amúġa. Tá beaṫa na nGaoḋal ċoṁ truaiġe, ċoṁ dub doiliġ dobrónaċ sin, agus tá siad ċoṁ brisde brúiġte buailte-síos ann a dtír agus a dtalaṁ féin, naċ bfágann a n-inntleaċt agus a ngeur-inntinn aon áit dóiḃ féin, ná aon tsliġe le iad féin do leigean amaċ, aċt i ngáire agus i ngreann iomarcaċ amadánta, no i g-caointib agus i g-cúṁa. Feicfimid ann sna dántaiḃ seo leanas, níos mó de brón agus de ḃuairḋreaḋ, níos mó de cúṁa agus de ċroiḋe-ḃrúiġteaċt, 'ná de ġreannaṁlaċt agus de ḋóṫċas. Aċt 'nn a aiṁḋeóin sin is cosṁúil gur b'iad na daoine ceudna, no an cineál ceudna de ḋaoinib, do rinne na dánta so leanas, agus na h-abráin sin do léiġeamar. Ní ṫig linn sin ċroṫuġaḋ, agus ní ḟeuċfamaoid a ċroṫuġaḋ, aċt cá bfuil an duine a bfuil fios aige air Ġaoḋaltaċt na h-Éireann ḋeurfas 'nn ár n'-aġaiḋ ann so.

Is fir do rinne na h-abráin uile ann san g-caibidil ḋeireannaiġ, aċt is mná do rinne cuid ṁaiṫ de na h-abránaiḃ gráḋa agus is go binn brónaċ rinneadar iad. Cad é an teanga ann a bfuiġfimid fíor-ḋórtaḋ croiḋe brónaiġ buḋ ṁillse agus buḋ ṁó cúṁa 'ná ann san abrán so, do rinne maiġdean éigin do

FOURTH CHAPTER.

LOVE SONGS.

AFTER reading these wild, careless, sporting, airy drinking-songs, it is right that a chapter entirely contrary to them should follow. Not careless and light-hearted alone is the Gaelic nature, there is also beneath the loudest mirth a melancholy spirit, and if they let on (pretend) to be without heed for anything but sport and revelry, there is nothing in it but letting on (pretence). The same man who will to-day be dancing, sporting, drinking and shouting, will be soliloquising by himself to-morrow, heavy and sick and sad in his poor lonely little hut, making a croon over departed hopes, lost life, the vanity of this world, and the coming of death. There is for you the Gaelic nature, and that person who would think that they are not the same sort of people who made those loud-tongued, sporting, devil-may-care songs that we have been reading in the last chapter, and who made the truly gentle, smooth, fair, loving poems which he will see in this part, is very much astray. The life of the Gaels is so pitiable, so dark and sad and sorrowful, and they are so broken, bruised, and beaten down in their own land and country that their talents and ingenuity find no place for themselves, and no way to let themselves out but in excessive foolish mirth, or in keening and lamentation. We shall see in these poems that follow, more grief, and trouble, more melancholy and contrition of heart, than of gaiety or hope. But despite that, it is probably the same men, or the same class of men who composed the poems which follow and the songs which we have read. We cannot prove that, and we shall not try to prove it, but where is the person who knows the Gaeldom of Erin and will say against (*i.e.* contradict) us in this.

They were men who composed all the songs in the last chapter, but it is women who made many of the love songs, and melodious and sorrowful they made them. In what language will we find the real out-pouring of a sorrowful heart, sweeter and more melancholy than this song, which some maiden composed who gave her love to a man

ṫug grád d'ḟear nár ṫuig é. Tá ainm an ċailín caillte, agus ní 'l ḟios air an ócáid air a n-dearnaid sí an dán so, na ar aon rud eile d'á ṫaoib, acht aṁáin go bfuil an dán féin ann sin. Sin í an ċaoi le trí ceaṫraṁnaiḃ agus níos mó de na dántaiḃ ann san leaḃar so; ní ṁaireann de na daoiniḃ do ċum iad faoi ḃrón agus faoi ġeur-ċrád acht na h-abráin,

Is buaine port na glór na n-eun
Is buaine focal na toice an tsaéġail.

Ag so an dán do rinne sí, agus is follasaċ gur cailín-tuaiṫe ḃí innti.

DÁ DTÉIḊINN-SE SIAR.

Dá dtéiḋinn-se siar is aniar ní ṫiucfainn,
Air an g-cnoc do b'áirde is air a ḟeasfainn,
'S í an ċraoḃ ċúṁarṫa is túirse* ḃainfinn
'Gus is é mo ġrád féin as luaiṫe leanfainn.

Tá mo ċroiḋe ċoṁ duḃ le áirne,
Ná le gual duḃ ḋóiġfiḋe i g-ceartaiḋ,
Le bonn bróige air hállaiḋiḃ bána,
'S tá lionnduḃ mór os cionn mo ġáire

Tá mo ċroiḋe-se brúiġte briste,
Mar leac-oiḋre air uaċtar uisge,
Mar beiḋ' cnuasaċ cnó léis† a mbriste,
Ná maiġdean óg léis a pósta.

Ta mo ġrád-sa air ḋaṫ na sméara,
'S air ḋaṫ na súġ-craoḃ, lá breáġ gréine,
Air ḋaṫ na bfraoċóg duḃ duiḃe an tsléiḃe,
'Gus is minic ḃí ceann duḃ air ċollainn gléġil.

Is mitid daṁ-sa an baile seó ḟágḃáil,
Is geur an ċloċ 'gus is fuar an láib ann,
Is ann a fuaireas guṫ gan éadáil,
Agus focal trom ó luċt an ḃiodáin.

---

* Aliter, "is taoisge" = is luaiṫe.

† .i. 's éis, no, tar éis. Labartar é i g-condaé Roscomáin agus i n-áiteaċaiḃ eile mar "léis."

who did not understand it. The girl's name, and the occasion on which she made this poem, and everything else about it, is unknown, except that the poem is here. That is the way with three-fourths and more of the poems in this book; there remains nothing of the people who composed them in grief and tribulation, except the songs.

A tune is more lasting than the voice of the birds,
A word is more lasting than the riches of the world.

This is the poem she made, and it is evident that she was a country girl.

IF I WERE TO GO WEST.

If I were to go west, it is from the west I would not come,
On the hill that was highest, 't is on it I would stand,
It is the fragrant branch I would soonest pluck,
And it is my own love I would quickest follow.

My heart is as black as a sloe,
Or as a black coal that would be burnt in a forge,
As the sole of a shoe upon white halls,
And there is great melancholy over my laugh.

My heart is bruised, broken,
Like ice upon the top of water,
As it were a cluster of nuts after their breaking,
Or a young maiden after her marrying.

My love is of the colour of the blackberries,
And the colour of the raspberry on a fine sunny day.
Of the colour of the darkest heath-berries of the mountain,
And often has there been a black head upon a bright body

Time it is for me to leave this town,
The stone is sharp in it, and the mould is cold;
It was in it I got a voice (blame), without riches
And a heavy word from the band who back-bite.

Fuagraim an gráḋ, is mairg do ṫug é
Do ṁac na mná úd, ariaṁ nár ṫuig é,
Mo ċroiḋe ann mo lár gur ḟágḃuiḋ sé duḃ é,
'S ni ḟeicim air an tsráid ná i n-áit air biṫ é.

Sin aḃráñ naċ féidir a ḟáruġaḋ air ṡimpliḋeaċt air ṁine agus caoine agus air ḋoḃrón doiṁin. Ag sin mar fuair mise é, aċt tá dá rann eile ann, do ḃí deunta le duine eile gan amras, ciḋ go ḃfuair siad áit ann san dán so. Tá an inġean ag laḃairt le na máṫair ann san g-ceud rann, agus tá an dara inġean ag laḃairt leis an máṫair ann san dara rann.

(An ċeud inġean ag laḃairt fós.)

A ṁáiṫrín ḋileas taḃair mé féin ḋó,
Taḃair na baċ a's na caoiriġ go léir ḋó,
Téiḋ, ṫu féin, ag iarraiḋ na déirce
A's ná gaḃ siar na aniar dom' éiliuġaḋ.

(An dara inġean ag cur na h-aġaiḋ.)

A ṁáṫairín ḋileas taḃair í féin dó,
Ná taḃair na baċ ná na caoiriġe go léir dó,
Ná téiḋ ṫu fein ag iarraiḋ na déirce
D'aon ṁac bodaiġ d'á ḃfuil beó i n-Éirinn.

Ḃeirim an dá rann so, aċt sgaoilim ó'n gcuid eile de'n dán iad, óir is follasaċ gur duine éigin eile do ċuir i g-cionn an máṫair-aḃráin iad.

Ag sin an bean ag taḃairt sóláis d'á croiḋe briste, le na smuainte do ċur i ḃfoclaiḃ. Seó anois an fear ag iarraiḋ an rud ceudna do ḋeunaṁ, agus doilġeas doiṁin doḃrónaċ agus cúṁa cruaiḋ cráiḋte air. Is é is ainm do'n aḃrán so, Mala Néifin. Ċualaiḋ mé cuid dé ó ṁnaoi i g-Condaé Roscomáin, agus tá aon rann aṁáin dé i leaḃar Ui h-Argadáin, aċt ní ḃfuair mé ariaṁ cóip iomlán dé no go ḃfuair mé ann san t-sean-láimsgríbinn é, as ar ḃain mé an oiread sin d'aḃránaiḃ ċeana. Níor ḟeud mé aon ċóip dé d'ḟáġail ann sna MSS. 'san Ārd-sgoil Ríoġaṁuil Eireannaiġ. Is cosṁúil gur sine go mór an dán so 'ná aon niḋ an Ċearḃallánaiġ. Is sliaḃ a ḃfad siar i g-Condaé Ṁuiġ-eó, Néifin, agus is é an sliaḃ do ṫug ainm do'n aḃrán. Is

I denounce love ; woe is she who gave it
To the son of yon woman, who never understood it.
My heart in my middle, sure he has left it black,
And I do not see him on the street or in any place.

That is a song that cannot be surpassed for simplicity, softness, gentleness, and deep sorrow. That is how I found it; but there are two other verses that were, without doubt, composed by some one else, though they have found a place in this poem. The daughter is speaking to her mother in the first verse, and the second daughter is speaking to the mother in the second verse.

THE FIRST DAUGHTER SPEAKS.

Oh! dear little mother, give him myself;
Give him the cows and the sheep altogether.
Go yourself a-begging alms,
And go not west or east to look for me.

THE SECOND DAUGHTER (OPPOSING).

Oh! dear little mother, give him herself;
Do not give him the cows and the sheep altogether.
Do not go yourself begging for alms
For any son of churl who is alive in Erin.

I give these two verses, but I separate them from the rest of the poem, for it is evident that it was some other person who added them to the mother-song.

There is the woman seeking satisfaction for her broken heart by putting her thoughts into words. Here, now, is the man trying to do the same thing in deep, mournful sorrow, and hard and ruined (*i.e.*, ruinous) melancholy upon him. The name of this song is the "Brow of Nephin." I heard part of it from a woman in Roscommon, and there is one verse of it given in Hardiman's book; but I never got a complete copy of it until I found it in my old manuscript, out of which I have already taken so many songs. I was unable to find any copy of it in the MSS. in the Royal Irish Academy. It is likely that this poem is older than anything of Carolan's. Nephin is a mountain far west in the county Mayo, and the mountain gave its name to the song. No doubt it was a peasant who was neither poet or bard who com-

dóiġ gur duine-tíre naċ raiḃ 'nna file ná 'nna ḃárd do rinne é, aċt is beag d'aḃránaiḃ na mbárd mór atá—dar liom-sa—ċom milis leis.

Mala Néifin.

Dá mbéiḋinn-se air Ṁala Néifin
'S mo ċeud-ġráḋ le mo ṫaoiḃ,*
Is láġaċ ċoideólamaois i n-éinfeaċt
Mar an t-éinín air an g-craoiḃ.
'Sé do ḃéilín binn briaṫraċ
Do ṁeudaiġ air mo ṗian,
Agus codlaḋ ciúin ní ḟeudaim,
Go n-éugfad, faraor!

Dá mbéiḋinn-se air na cuantaiḃ
Mar buḋ dual dam, ġeoḃainn spórt,
Mo ċáirde uile faoi ḃuaiḋreaḋ
Agus gruaim orra gaċ ló.
Fíor-sgaiṫ na ngruagaċ
Fuair buaiḋ a's clú anns gaċ gleó,
'S gur b'é mo ċroiḋe-stiġ tá 'nna ġual duḃ,
Agus bean mo ṫruaiġe ní'l beó.

Naċ aoiḃinn do na h-éininiḃ
A éiriġeas go h-árd,
'S a ċodluiġeas i n-éinfeaċt
Air aon ċraoiḃín aṁáin.
Ní mar sin dam féin
A's do m' ċeud míle gráḋ
Is fada o na ċéile orrainn
Éiriġeas gaċ lá.†

---

* "Beiṫ agam," i n-áit "le mo ṫaoiḃ," 'san MS.

† Aliter.

Ní hé sin féin daṁ-sa
Ná do m' ċeud míle gráḋ,
Is fada fánaċ ó na ċéile
Bíos air n-éiriġe gaċ lá.

posed it, but there are few songs of the great bards themselves that are in my opinion as sweet as it.

THE BROW OF NEFIN.*

Did I stand on the bald top of Néfin
  And my hundred-times loved one with me,
We should nestle together as safe in
  Its shade as the birds on a tree.
From your lips such a music is shaken,
  When you speak it awakens my pain,
And my eyelids by sleep are forsaken,
  And I seek for my slumber in vain.

But were I on the fields of the ocean,
  I should sport on its infinite room,
I should plough through the billow's commotion
  Though my friends should look dark at my doom.
For the flower of all maidens of magic
  Is beside me where'er I may be,
And my heart like a coal is extinguished,
  Not a woman takes pity on me.

How well for the birds in all weather,
  They rise up on high in the air
And then sleep upon one bough together
  Without sorrow or trouble or care;
But so it is not in this world
  For myself and my thousand-times fair,
For away, far apart from each other,
  Each day rises barren and bare.

---

* LITERAL TRANSLATION.

If I were to be on the Brow of Nefin and my hundred loves by my side, it is pleasantly we would sleep together like the little bird upon the bough. It is your melodious wordy little mouth that increased my pain, and a quiet sleep I cannot (get) until I shall die, alas!

If I were to be on the harbours as I ought to be, I would get sport, my friends all under trouble and gloom upon them every day.

O thou flower (?) of enchanters who got victory and fame in every strife, sure it is my heart within that is a black coal and a woman of my pity (*i.e.*, to pity me) lives not.

Is it not delightful for the little birds who rise up high and who sleep together upon one little bough? Not so is it for me myself and my hundred thousand loves, it is far from each other each day rises on us.

What is your opinion of the sky when there comes a heat upon the day, or on the full tide rising in the face of the high ditch? Even so does he be who gives excessive desire to love, like a tree on the brow of a mountain which its blossoms would forsake.

Cad é do ḃreaċnuġaḋ air na spéarṫaiḃ
Traṫ [ṫig] teas air an lá,
Na air an lán-mara ag éiriġe
Le h-eudan an ċloiḋe áird?
Mar súd bíos an té úd
A ḃeir an-toil do 'n ġráḋ
Mar ċrann air ṁala sléiḃe
Do* ṫréigfeaḋ a bláṫ.

Tar éis an dá abrán mí-ṁisneaṁuil seó do ṫabairt, leanfamaoid iad le dá abrán eile de ċineál contrárḋa, abráin d'feudfainn ċur asteaċ ameasg abrán-molta-na-mban aċt gur sean abráin gráḋ iad air feaḋ Eireann air fad, agus beirim ann so cóip Ċonnaċtaċ do fuair mé ann san tsean sgríbinn air ar labair mé ċoṁ minic seo, agus cóip Ṁuiṁneaċ do fuair mé i láiṁ-sgríbinn do rinn an ríġ-sgoláire Gaeḋeilg sin Dóṁnall Mac Consaidin o Innis i g-condaé an Chláir. Is é an t-abrán so "Múirnín na gruaige báine." Tá an ċeud ċóip cosṁúil leis an té sin atá ag an h-Argadánaċ, aċt ní'l sí ċoṁ cosṁúil léiṫe naċ fiú a sabáil. Ag so é.

Múirnín na gruaige báine,

'S i mbaile-na-hinnse ṫiar
Atá mo ġráḋ le bliaḋain,
Is áille í 'ná grian an ḟóġṁair,
'S go bḟásann mil 'nna diaiġ
Air lorg a cos 'san tsliaḃ
Dá ḟuaire an uair 'réir na Saṁna.
Dá bḟáġainn féin mo ṁian†
Go ngabainn í ann mo líon

* "Ann do ṫréigfead," 'san MS., aċt ni ḟeicim bríġ an "ann" so.

† "Dá bḟaġainn ar staid mo ċiall," 'san MS. B'éidir = "Dá bḟágfainn ar stáid [bean] mo ċiall" .i. mo rún no mo ṫoil.

Say, what dost thou think of the heavens
When the heat overmasters the day,
Or what when the steam of the tide
Rises up in the face of the bay?
Even so is the man who has given
An inordinate love-gift away,
Like a tree on a mountain all riven
Without blossom or leaflet or spray.

After giving these two dispirited songs we will follow them with two other songs of a contrary kind, songs which I might have included amongst those in praise of women, except that they are old love songs throughout the length and breadth of Ireland, and I give here a Connacht copy which I found in the old manuscript about which I have spoken so often, and a Munster copy which I found in a manuscript of mine which that fine Irish scholar, Donal MacConsadine, from Ennis, in the county Clare, made. This song is the "Moorneen (darling) of the fair hair." This first version is like that which the Hargadaunuch (Hardiman) has, but it is not so like it that it is not worth while to save it. Here it is—

THE MOORNEEN, OR DARLING, OF THE FAIR HAIR.

In Ballinahinch in the West
My love is for a year,
She is more exquisite than the sun of the autumn,
And, sure, honey grows after her,
On the track of her foot on the mountains,
No matter how cold the time after November.

A's go g-cuirfinn-se an brón so ḋíom ó'n lá sin †
A's air ċómairle a rugaḋ riaṁ
Ní ṗósfaiḋ mé aċt mo ṁian
Is í Ṁúirnín na gruaige báine.

Tá mo ċeuċta le sgur
A's mo ḃranrra le cur
Agus an méad úd uile le deunaṁ,
Mé do ḃeiṫ amuiġ
Air ḟearṫainn a's air ṡioc
Air súil go dtiúbrá spéis dam.

Is coma leat é
A ċaraid o mo ċléiḃ,
Ní ort atá an ṗian ċráidte,
Agus dúiṫċe flaiṫeas Dé
Nár ḟeicfiḋ tu go h-éug
Muna dtugaiḋ do ċroiḋe-stiġ ġráḋ dam.

Dá ḃfáġainn-se mo roġa
De ṁnáiḃ deasa an domain,
Agus fáġaim orra roġain fásta,
Agus réir mar deir na leaḃair
Do ṫug sí buaiḋ ó'n doṁan
Is í Múirnín na gruaige báine.

Seó anois an cóip Ṁuiṁneaċ mar d'ḟág Mac Consaidín 'nna ḋiaiġ í, agus adṁuiġim go toilteannaċ gur fearr í 'ná an ceann ṡuas.

MÁIRE ḂHEAG NA GRUAIGE BÁINE.

Cois na Ḃríġde síar atá mo ġráḋ le bliaḋain
A saṁuil súd mar ġrian an tsaṁraiḋ,
Fásann mil 'nna diaiġ air lorg a cos san tsliab
Seaċt seaċtṁuine tar éis na Saṁna.
Dá ḃfáġainn-se féin a tuairisg 's í bean an ċúilín ḋualaiġ
An ainnir úd do luaiḋeaḋ air ḃreáġaċt,
'S gur ag geataiḃ Ċill-dá-luaċ do sgaras-sa le m'uan
Is í Máire na gruaige báine.

---

† "Gan buaiḋreaḋ" 'san MS, dá ḟocal ġníḋeas droċ-ḟuaim.

If I were myself to get my desire,
Sure I would take her in my net,
  And I would put away from me this grief without trouble.
And for the counsel of all ever were born
I shall only marry my desire,
  She is the Moorneen of the fair hair.

My plough is to cease,
And my lea-land to sow,
  And all that is to be done;
Me to be out
In rain and in frost
  In hope that you would give me liking.

It is all one to you
Oh! friend of my bosom;
  Not on you is the ruinous pain (*but on me*),
And the country of the heavens of God
That you may never see till death,
  Unless the inner heart give me love.

If I were to get my choice
Of the pretty women of the world,
  And let me get of them a satisfactory choice (*I would take you*).
And as the books say
She took the victory from the world,
  She is the Moorneen of the fair hair.

Here, now, is the Munster version as Considine left it after him, and I willingly admit that it is better than the one just given.

LITTLE MARY OF THE FAIR HAIR.

Beside the Breed in the West, my love is for a year.
  Her likeness is as the sun of the summer.
Honey grows behind her on the track of her feet in the mountain
  Seven weeks after November day (i.e., *even in the heart of winter*)
If I were myself to get her description she is the woman of the
    tressy cooleen,
  Yonder maiden who was spoken of (or betrothed) for loveliness,
And sure at the gates of Killaloe I parted with my lamb,
  She is Maurya (Mary) of the fair hair.

Nár ṫigeaḋ-sa féin do'n éag no seal fé ḃárr an ḟéir
   Is cúṁa as do ḃéiġ ní náir liom,
Aċt codlaḋ air nós na n-éun i mbárr bog na gcraoḃ
   No an ḃfuil 'aon ḟear a bpéin mar táim-se.
Dá ḟad í an oiḋċe 'réir níor ċodail mo súile neul,
   Aċt ag maċtnaṁ air ġníoṁarṫaiḃ Ṁaire,
A's go bráṫ nár ṫagaiḋ an t-eug i mbárr fuar mo ġéag
   Go ḃfeicfeaḋ-sa i dtiġeas mo ġráḋ geal.

Cois na ḃríġde móire atá mo ṁíle stór-sa
   'S í an ainḋir tá móḋaṁuil beusaċ,
'S gur millse blas a póg 'ná súcra beaċ air bórd,
   'S a ḃeiṫ d'á ól air ḃrannda craosag.*
Ḋá ċíċ ḃreaġa ḋeasa ḃána ṁíne ġeala
   Mar eala ḃeiḋeaḋ air an linn 'nna h-aonar,
A's go laḃarann an ċuaċ air lár an ġeiṁriḋ ḟuair
   'S an mbaile mbeag 'nna mbíonn sí pléireaċt.

Naċ doilḃ duḃaċ an cás do ḋuine mar atáim
   Nac g-cuiriḋ na mná so suim ann,
'S gur b'é ċluinim-se dá ráḋ go dtaḃarfaidís súd gráḋ
   Do'n ḟear is measa cáil i n-Éirinn.
Naċ raḃad* ann arís go dtógfad mo lion
   A's go mbainfinn-se d'á gcroiḋe súd sásaṁ,
Tar a maireann beó de ṁnáiḃ, is í súd mo ġráḋ,
   Máire ḃeag na gruaige báine.

Dá sgríoḃfainn an t-abrán 'san rannaiġeaċt agus 'san miosúr ceudna leis an g-ceann deiríonnaċ d'ḟeicfiḋe é go foṡar ċoṁ cos-ṁúil le ċéile atá siad. Aċt atá cóip eile, cóip Ṁuiṁneaċ as sgríbinn do rinne an Consaidín ceudna, agus sgríoḃfaiḋ mé é 'san rannaiġeaċt ċeudna 'nn ar sgríobas an dán Connaċtaċ, go saṁlóċamaoid le ċéile níos fearr iad. Aċt ní mar sin fuair mé é sgroḃṫa leis an g-Consaidín aċt le líntiḃ fada, mar an "Ṁáire ḃeag na gruaige báine," ṡuas.

---

*=Caor-ḋearg, ċom dearg le caor.
*=Ná raiḃ mé (?)

That I may never come to the death or a while beneath the earth's
top
And melancholy after thee I think no shame,
But sleep like the birds in the soft top of the boughs,
Or is any man in pain as I am ?
No matter how long last night was, my eyes never slept a wink
But musing on the deeds of Maurya,
And that the Death may never come in the cold top of my branches
Until I see my white love in a household.

Beside the great Breed my thousand treasures is,
She is the maiden who is mannerly, courteous,
And sure the taste of her'kisses is sweeter than the honey of the
bees on the table
And to be drinking it in berry-red brandy.
Two breasts—fine, handsome, white, smooth, bright,
Like a swan that would be alone upon the linn ;
And sure the cuckoo speaks in the middle of the cold winter
In the little village in which she is sporting.

Is it not sorrowful, mournful, the case to a person as I am
That these women pay him no attention ?
And sure what I hear said is that they would give their love
To the man of the worst character in Erin.
That I may not be in it again until I lift up my net
And until I take satisfaction out of their hearts,
Over all that live of women she yonder is my love,
Little Maurya of the fair hair.

If I were to write this song in the same metre and measure as the last one it would easily be seen how like they are to one-another. But there exists another version, a Munster one from a manuscript of mine which the same Considine made, and I shall write it in the same measure as I wrote the Connacht song, that we may the better compare them with one another, but it was not thus I found it written by the Considine but in long lines like the " Mary of the Fair Hair," above.

Múirnín na gruaige báine.

Mo léun gan mé 'gus tu
A ṁaiġdean óg gan ċúṁ'
I n-oileánaiḃ duḃa Loċ' Eirne,
No faoi ċoilltiḃ duḃ' na slat
Mar a ndeunaid na h-éanlaiṫ nead
Agus fásaċ go bárra geuga.
No i ngleanntáinín cois cuain
Mar a labrann an ċuaċ,
A's an fairrge o ṫuaiṫ beiṫ taoḃ linn,
Mise féin 's mo rún
Gan codlaḋ ann nó suan
Aċt ag súgraḋ i g-clúid a ċéile.

Mo leun! gan mé 'sa' g-cill
I ḃfoċair mo ċáirde gaoil
No i mullaċ cnuic ag deunaṁ áruis
Sul fá r' ṫárla tu am' líon
Ag dúbailt cnead am' ċroiḋe
Agus d'iompuiġ tu mo ḋlaoiġ mar áirne.
Cumann gear[r]* o ṁnaoi
Ní ṁaireann sé aċt mí
Aċt mar ṡiolla de ġaoiṫ Ṁárta,
A stóir níor ċóir mé ḋíol
Mar ġeall air beagán maoin'
A's fearta liom bíoḋ d'inntinn sásta.

Níor ḟág mé baile cuain
O Ċorcaiġ anuas
No as sin go Cruaċ-Pádraig
Ṫart ó ḋeas anuas
Go béul an Easa Ruaiḋ
Nár ċaiṫeas, air mo ċuairt ann, páiṫċe.
Mar súil go ḃfáġainn tuairisg
Ṗéurla an ċúil dualaiġ
'S í an ainnir do ṫug buaiḋ ṫar ṁnáiḃ í,
'S gur i dteórainn Ċill-dá-lua
Do sgaras le mo rún
Is í Múirnín na gruaige báine.

---

* Ní'l ḟios agam an é seó "géur," no "gearr."

THE MOORNEEN OF THE FAIR HAIR.

[MUNSTER VERSION].

My grief that I and thou
Oh young maiden without melancholy
Are not in the dark island of Lough Erne,
Or beneath the dark woods of the rods,
Where the birds make their nests
And (there is) growth to the top of the boughs.
Or in a little valley beside a bay
Where the cuckoo speaks,
And the sea from the north to be beside us,
Myself and my secret
Without sleep or slumber
But playing in a corner together.

My grief that I am not in the church-yard
Along with my kindred friends,
Or on the top of a hill making a dwelling,
Before you chanced into my net
Doubling the wound in my heart,
And you turned my locks like a sloe-berry.
Short affection from a woman
It only lasts a month,
But it is like a whiff of the March wind,
Oh treasure, it were not right to sell me
On account of a little riches
And in future let your mind be satisfied with me.

I never left a harbour town
From Cork down
Nor from that to Croagh Patrick (in Mayo),
Round from the south, and down
To the mouth of the Red Waterfall (*i.e.*, Ballyshanon),
That I did not spend a quarter-of-a-year on my visit in it,
In hopes that I might get an account
Of the pearl of the tressy *cool*;
She is the maiden who gained the victory over women.
And sure at the mearn of Killaloe
I parted with my secret,
She is the Moorneen of the fair hair.

Cois na h-aibne móire
Atá mo ṁíle stóraċ
'S í an ṁaiġdean ṁaiseaċ ṁo[ḋ]ṁ[a]raċ fásta í,
'S go mbuḋ ṁillse liom a póg
'Ná mil na mbeaċ air bórd,
Agus í do ḃeiṫ 'gá h-ól le brannda.
A ḋá ċíċ ċruinne ḃreáġa
Cumṫa deasa bláṫṁar'
Mar ḃeideaḋ sneaċta 'gá ċaṫaḋ air ḟléiḃtiḃ,
'S go labrann an ċuaċ le fonn
Air lár an ġeiṁriḋ ṫall
'San mbaile 'nna mbíonn mo ġráḋ le pléisiúr.

Tá aon ḃeursa eile ann san abrán, aċt is dóiġ liom naċ mbaineann sé leis, agus gur duine éigin eile do rinne é, aċt ḃéarfad ann so é.

Tá cuid aca dá ráḋ
Gur mór mo ġean air ṁnáiḃ
Níor ṫugas-sa mo ġean aċt do ċúigear,
A's i g-contabairt mo ḃáṫaḋ*
Go leanfainn ṫu 'sa' snáṁ
D'ḟonn ḃeiṫ ann do ṗáirt a ċúil-ḟionn.
Do ḃeunfainn páirt de luing
'S do stiúróċainn í tar tuinn
Do ṡníoṁfainn gad 's do ḋeunfainn céuċta,
Mo leanabán beag fionn
Do ḃreugfainn í air mo ġlúin,
A's go raċfainn seal faoi ḃeinn a léine.

Cassamaoid anois air abrán dobrónaċ eile, do rinne maiġdean óg ag deunaṁ cúṁa agus liondub andiaiġ a gráḋ-sa. Chualaiḋ mé cuid dé ó ṡean-ṁnaoi i g-condaé Ṡligiġ, aċt ḃí sé fuaiṫe agus measgṫa le droċ-ḃéursaiḃ eile, agus ar an ádbar sin ḃeirim cuid dé as an láiṁ-sgríḃinn agus cuid eile naċ ḃfuil 'san láiṁ-sgríḃinn mar fuair mé ó'n tsean-ṁnaoi é. Tá an ċeud ḃeursa agus an ceann deirionnaċ ó'n tsean ṁnaoi, agus na tri cinn eile ó'n MS.

---

* B'ḟearr "mo ḃáiḋte."

Beside the great river
Is my thousand treasures,
She is the maiden—handsome, mannerly, satisfying ;
And sure her kiss was sweeter to me
Than the honey of the bees at table,
And it to be drunk with brandy.
Her two breasts—round, fine,
Shapen, handsome, blossomy—
As it were snow that would be thrown on mountains;
And sure the cuckoo speaks with delight
In the middle of the winter over there
In the village in which my love doth be with pleasure.

There is one other verse in the song, but I am sure it does not belong to it, and that it was somebody else who made it, but I shall give it here :—

There are some of them saying
That my love for women is great
But I never gave it but to five ;
And, in danger of being drowned,
Sure I would follow you in the ocean
With desire to be in your part (*i.e.*, dear to you), oh fair-haired one!
I would make portion of a ship,
And I would steer it across the waves ;
I would spin a gad (withy), and I would make a plough,
My little fair child
I would coax her on my knee,
And sure I would go awhile beneath the corner of her mantle.

We shall now meet another mournful song which a young maiden composed lamenting and grieving after her love. I heard part of it from an old woman in the county Sligo, but it was mixed up and mingled with other bad verses, and for that reason I give part of it out of my manuscript and part that is not in the manuscript, as I got it from the old woman. The first verse and the last are from her and the other three from the manuscript :—

Mala an tSléiḃe Ruaiḋ.

Tá mé ann mo ṡuiḋe
    O d'éiriġ an ġealaċ aréir,
Ag cur teineaḋ sios
    Agus go síor 'gá ḟadóġaḋ go ġeur,
Tá muinntir an tiġe
    'Nna luiḋe agus mise liom féin,
Tá na coilliġe ag glaoḋaċ
    Agus an tír 'nna codlaḋ aċt mé.

Ná'r ḟágḃuiġ mé an saoġal so
    Go sgaoilfiḋ mé díom an mí-áḋ,
Go raiḃ baċ agam agus caoiriġe
    A's mo ṁian de ḃuaċaill aṁáin,
Níor ḃfada liom an oiḋċe
    Ḃeiḋinn sinte le na ḃrollaċ min bán
'S go dtiúḃrainn cead do ṡíol Éaḃa
    'Nna ḋiaiġ sin a roġa rud a ráḋ.

Ḟoluiġeann gráḋ gráin
    Ann gaċ áit a m bíonn maise 'san mnaoi
Air leabaiḋ caol árd
    Le páiṫċe níor ḃfada mo luiḋe,
Nuair ċuiṁniġ mé air mo ġráḋ
    D'ḟág mé air ṁala an tsléiḃe ruaiḋ
Goilim mo ṡáiṫ
    'Gus is fánaċ ċiormuiġeas mo ġruaiḋ.

An lionduḃ a ġniḋim féin
    Ní ḟeudaim dadaiḋ ḋé ól,
Is measa mar táim
    Ní ḟeudaim codlaḋ go fóil,*
Mallaċt Ṁic Dé do'n té sin
    Do ḃain díom mo ġráḋ,
Agus d'ḟágḃuiġ liom féin mé
    Gaċ aon oiḋċe fada fá ċráḋ†

---

* "An codlaḋ a ḟáġail," 'san MS.
† "Fá ḃrón," 'san MS.

THE BROW OF THE RED MOUNTAIN.

I am sitting up
Since the moon rose last night,
And putting down a fire,
And ever kindling it diligently;
The people of the house
Are lying down, and I by myself.
The cocks are crowing,
And the land is asleep but me.

That I may never leave the world
Till I loose from me the ill-luck,
Till I have cows and sheep
And my one desire of a boy.
I would not think the night long
That I would be stretched by his smooth white breast,
And sure I would allow the race of Eve
After that to say their choice thing (*of me*).

Love covers up hate
In every place in which there is beauty in a woman
On a couch narrow, high,
For a quarter-of-a-year great and long (*was I*) lying,
When I remembered my love
That I left on the Brow of the Red Mountain,
I weep my enough
And it is scarcely (?) my countenance dries.

The grief (*or black ale, a play on words*) I myself make
I cannot drink any of it ;
It is worse as I am
I cannot get the sleep;
The curse of the Son of God upon that one
Who took from me my love
And left me by myself
Each single long night in misery.

'S a ḃuaċaillín óig
    ní áḋḃar air biṫ magaiḋ ḋuit mé,
Níl agad le ráḋ
    Aċt aṁáin go ḃfuil mé gan spré,
Ní tusa mo ġráḋ
    Agus mo ċráḋ má's miste liom é,
'S má tá mé gan ḃólaċt
    Is leór ḋam laiḋe* liom féin.

Tá an t-aḃrán so an-doḃrónaċ, mar an ċuid is mó de na h-aḃránaiḃ gráḋ tá deunta le mnáiḃ, agus tá an fonn. níos doḃrónaiġe 'ná na focail féin. Tá sé an-ċosṁúil le h-aḃrán ar an ḃfonn ceudna do fuair mé i láiṁsgríḃinn Ṁuiṁniġ le Dóṁnall Mac Consaidín. Is dóiġ go ḃfuair seisean an dán ó ḟean-duine éigin agus gur sgríoḃ sé síos é. Ciḋ gur i sgríḃinn Ṁuiṁniġ do fuair mé é, ní i g-cúige Muṁan aṁáin atá sé le fáġail, mar ċualas cuid dé i g-Connaċtaiḃ, mé féin. Is de na h-aḃranaiḃ sin é atá coitċionn do'n dá ċúige. Is cailín atá ann so arís ag deunaṁ bróin dí féin fá naċ dtig léiṫe a roġa-ġráḋ féin ḃeiṫ aici Tá sé an-ċosṁúil leis an aḃrán air a nglaoḋann oDálaiġ Caisleán Ui Néill, aċt tá ḃeursaiḋ ann so naċ ḃfuil aige-sean, agus ar an áḋḃar sin creidim gur fiú a ṫaḃairt ann so.†

AN TUIRSE A'S AN BRÓN SO.

Tá an tuirse a's an brón so
    Ag gabail go mór mór timċioll mo ċroiḋe,
A's lán mo ḋá ḃróga dé
    'S na deóra ag sileaḋ liom síos.
'S é is fada liom uaim an Dóṁnaċ
    A ṁíle stóirín no go ngaḃann tu an tsliġe
Agus m' annsaċt fá ḋó ṫu,
    Slán beó leat no go ḃfillfiḋ mé arís.

A ċumainn a's a annsaċt
    I dtúis an tsaṁraiḋ an ngluaisfeá liom féin,
Amaċ faoi na gleanntaiḃ
    Mar a mbeiḋmís ag dul faoi do'n ġréin.
Ba, caoirige, ná géana
    Ni iarrfainn leat iad mar spré,
Aċt mo láṁ faoi do ċom ġeal
    A's cead cóṁráḋ no go mbuailfeaḋ an dó-deug.

*=luiḋe

† Feuc l. 82 de "Ḟiliḋeaċt na Cúige Múṁan," ii. cuid.

And oh, young *bohaleen*,
I am no material for mockery for you,
You have nothing to say
Except only that I am without a fortune.
You are not my love,
And my destruction if I am sorry for it ;
And if I am without cattle
It is enough for me (i.e., *I am able*) to lie alone.

This song is very sorrowful, like most of the love songs that are composed by women, and the air is more mournful than the words themselves. It is very like a song to the same air which I got in a Munster manuscript of mine by Donal Mac Consaidin. He probably got the poem from some old person and wrote it down. Although I found it in a Munster manuscript, it is not in Munster alone it is, for I heard some of it myself in Connacht. It is one of those songs that are common to the two provinces. It is again a girl who is here making lament for herself because she cannot have her choice love It is very like the song that O'Daly calls "Castle O'Neill," but there are verses here which he has not got, and for this reason I think it worth giving them here.

THIS WEARINESS AND GRIEF.

This weariness and grief
Are going greatly, greatly, round my heart,
And the full of my two shoes of it,
And the tears dropping down with me.
It is what I think the Sunday long from me,
Oh, thousand treasures till you pass the way.
And my darling twice over you are,
Giving farewell to you, until I return again.

Oh, affection, and oh, darling,
In the beginning of the summer would you move with me yourself
Out under (*i.e.*, among) the valleys,
Where we might be at the going-under of the sun (?)
Cows, sheep, or calves
I would not ask them for fortune with thee,
But my hand beneath your white form,
And leave to converse until twelve would strike.

Ceud slán do'n oiḋċe aréir
'S é mo leun naċ anoċt do ḃí air dtús
Ḃuaċaillín spéireaṁuil
Do ḃréugfaḋ mé seal air a ġlúin.
D'inneósainn féin sgeul duit,
Dá mb'ḟéidir go ndeunfá orm rún,
Go ḃfuil mo ġráḋ do m'ṫréigin
A Ḋia ġlégil 's a Ṁuire naċ truaġ!

Tig le fear beiṫ doḃrónaċ ċoṁ maiṫ le mnaoi. Ag so aḃrán beag simpliḋe do fuair mé o ḟean ḟear dar b'ainm O Falaṁain as Ḃaile-an-tobair.

IS FADA ME AG IMṪEAĊT.

Is fada mé ag imṫeaċt
Air ṫuairisg mná tiġe,
A tuairisg ní ḃfuaras
I mbaile no i dtír,
Nó go ḃfacaiḋ mé mo ṁúirnín
Air ṫaoiḃ Ċnuic na Siḋe,
A gruag na trí dualaċ
D'á sguabaḋ le gaoiṫ.

Is truaġ gan mé pósta
Le stór geal mo ċroiḋe,
Taoḃ ṫall de'n aḃainn ṁóir
Ná ag an gcloiḋe teóran le na taoiḃ.
Cuṁlódar* ban óg
Is iad a ṫógfaḋ mo ċroiḋe,
'S beiḋinn bliaḋain eile† di b' óige
Dá mbeiḋinn pósta ag mo ṁian.

Go ḃfásaiḋ dá sgiaṫán
As mo ċliaṫán anuas
'S go n-éirigim anáirde
Ameasg éinín an ċuain,
Go ndeuntar cóṁra ċláir ḋam
'S go dtéiḋ na tairngiḋe innti go dlúṫ,
Ní sgarfaiḋ do ġráḋ go bráṫ liom
Go mbéiḋ mé páiṫċe 'san uaiġ.

---

*=Cóṁluadar.

† Di b'óige=níos óige. Foirm Ċonnaċtaċ=ní b'óige.

A hundred farewells to last night ;
  It is my grief that it was not to-night that was first.
A sprightly *bohalcen*
  That would coax me awhile on his knee,
I would tell you a tale myself
  If it were possible you could keep a secret for me,
That my love is forsaking me,
  Oh ! bright God, and oh, Mary, is it not the pity !

A man can be sorrowful as well as a woman. Here is a little simple song I got from an old man named O'Fallon in Ballintubber.

LONG AM I GOING.

Long am I a-going
  Inquiring for a *ban-a-t'yee* (Hausfrau)
Information of her I did not get
  In town or in country.
Till I saw my darling
  On the side of the Fairy's Hill,
Her hair of the three tresses
  A-sweeping with wind.

'Tis a pity without me to be (*i.e.* that I am not) married.
  With the bright treasure of my heart,
On the brink by the great river
  Or at the nearer ditch by its side.
Company of young women,
  It is they who would raise my heart,
And I would be a year younger
  If I were married to my desire.

Until two wings grow
  Out of my two breasts,
And till I rise up on high
  Amongst the birds of the bay,
Till a coffin of boards is made for me
  And till the nails go closely into it,
Your love will never part me
  Until I shall be a quarter of a year in the tomb.

Air h-allaiḋiḃ an tiġe ṁóir-se
Cóṁnuiġeann a's bionn mo ġráḋ bán,
Air ḟad mo reult-eólais
'S é is dóiġ liom naċ mbíonn* sé le fáġail.
Buḋ ṁillse liom a ṗóigín
'Ná an beóir 's 'ná an siúcra bán
'S muna bfáġ' mé ṫu le pósaḋ
'S é is dóiġ liom naċ mbéiḋ mo ċroiḋe slán.

Atá an gáirdín seó 'nna ḟásaċ,
A ġráḋ ġeal, no an misde leat é?
Faoi na toraiḋibt breáġ' bána
Tá ag fás mar ḋuilleabar na g-craéḃ.
Níor binne liom glór céirsig
Ag gabail an tsráid seo ná guṫ binn na n-eun,
'S gur euluiġ mo ġráḋ uaim
Cúl fáinneaċ go Caisleán Ui Néill.

Is a m'sgeiċ i mbeul bearnan
Do fágbaḋ mé air maidin Dé Luain,
Gan aon duine beó i ndáil liom
Aċt mo ġráḋ bán a's é imṫiġṫe‡ a bfad uaim
Ni bfuil gile ná breáġaċt
Ná áilleaċt d'á raiḃ ann san ríoġaċt
Naċ bfuil ann mo ġráḋ bán
A's gur ḟág sé súd orna ann mo ċliaḃ.

Nár fágaiḋ mé an saoġal so
No go leigfiḋ mé ḋíom an mi-áḋ,
Go mbéiḋ baċ agam agus caoiriġe
Agus m'annsaċt air leabaiḋ go sáiṁ.
Trosgaḋ na h-Aoine
Ná lá saoire ni brisfinn go bráċ,
'S níor bfada liom an oiḋċe
Do beiḋinn sínte le d' ḃrollaċ geal bán.

---

* "Na biḋeann sé," san MS.
† "Faoi s na torraiḋe," 'san MS.—mar adeirid na Muiṁniġ.
‡ "Miṫe," 'san MS.

On the halls of this great house
  Resides and does be my white love,
Altogether (?) (*he is*) my knowledge-star;
  What I am sure of is that he is not to be got;
I would think his kiss sweeter
  Than the b'yore (*kind of beer*) and the sugar white;
And, unless I get you to marry,
  What I think certain is that my heart will not be whole.

This garden is a wilderness,
  Oh! white love; or, are you sorry for it?—
Under the fine white fruits
  That are growing like the foliage of the branches.
I would not think the voice of a thrush more sweet
  Going this street, or the melodious voice of the birds;
And sure my love has eloped from me,
  The ringletted *cool*, to the castle of O'Neill.

Like a (discarded) bush in the mouth of a gap
  I was left on Monday morning,
Without one person alive near me,
  But my white love—and he gone far from me.
There is no brightness nor fineness,
  Nor loveliness of all that were in the kingdom
That is not in my white love;
  And sure that left a sigh in my breast.

That I may never leave this world
  Till I let from me the ill-luck;
That I may have cows and sheep,
  And my affection on a couch pleasantly;
Fasting on Friday
  Or holiday I never would break;
And I would not think the night long
  That I would be near by your white bright heart.

Tá lúibín deas cúbarṫa agam
Air ċúl an ċnocáin,
Le mo ċúlḟionn do ḃreugaḋ
A's mo ċeud míle gráḋ.
Mar sin a ḃíḋeas mo ċroiḋe-se
Deunaṁ píosaiḋ ann mo lár,
Mar ḃeiḋeaḋ crann i lár sléiḃe
'S é gan fréaṁaiḃ ná croiḋe slán.

Mar ḃeiḋeaḋ* grian os cionn duiḃeaċáin
Bíonn m'inntinn, faraor!
Gan codlaḋ gan suaiṁneas
Le tuilleaḋ agus bliaḋain,
Is mar sin a ḃíḋeas mo ċroiḋe-se
Deunaṁ píosaiḋ ann mo lár,
Mar naċ dtigeann tu do m' iarraiḋ
Seal aon oiḋċe aṁáin.

Ag so mar ċaoineas bean anḋiaiġ a gráḋ-sa go fíor-ṡimpliḋe agus go h-an-ḃinn. Fuair mé an píosa so ó ḟean ṁnaoi dar b'ainm Ḃríġid ni Ċosruaiḋ† ḃí 'nna cóṁnuiḋe i mboṫán i lár por-taiġ i g-condaé Roscomáin agus í beag-naċ ceud bliaḋain d'aois.

MO ḂRÓN AIR AN ḂFAIRRGE.

Mo ḃrón air an ḃfairrge
Is é tá mór,
Is é gaḃail idir‡ mé
'S mo ṁíle stór.

D'ḟágaḋ 'san mbaile mé
Deunaṁ bróin,
Gan aon tsúil tar sáile liom
Coiḋċe na go deó.

---

* Labairtear an focal so mar "beiṫ," i n-aon siolla aṁáin, i g-Connaċtaiḃ.

† "Biddy Crummey," i m Beurla, Tá sí marḃ anois agus a cuid abrán léiṫe.

‡ Labairtear "idir" mar "eadar" i g-Conaċtaiḃ agus i n-Albainn.

I have a nice fragrant little corner (?)
  At the back of the hillock,
To entice my fair one
  And my hundred thousand loves.
Even so does my heart be,
  Making bits (of itself) in my middle,
As it were a tree in the midst of a mountain
  And it without roots or heart sound.

As it were a sun over an abyss
  My mind, alas, does be
Without sleep, without rest,
  For more than a year.
Even so my heart does be,
  Making pieces (of itself) in my middle,
Since thou comest not to seek me
  For a while of only one night.

This is how a woman keenes after her love, exceedingly simply, and melodiously. I got this piece from an old woman named Biddy Cussrooee (or Crummey in English), who was living in a hut in the midst of a bog in the County Roscommon.

* MY GRIEF ON THE SEA.

My grief on the sea,
  How the waves of it roll!
For they heave between me
  And the love of my soul!

Abandoned, forsaken,
  To grief and to care,
Will the sea ever waken
  Relief from despair?

---

* Literally. My grief on the sea, It is it that is big. It is it that is going between me And my thousand treasures. I was left at home Making grief, Without any hope of (going) over sea with me, For ever or aye. My grief that I am not, And my white moorneen, In the province of Leinster Or County of Clare. My sorrow I am not, And my thousand loves On board of a ship Voyaging to America: A bed of rushes Was under me last night And I threw it out With the heat of the day. My love came To my side, Shoulder to shoulder And mouth on mouth.

Mo léun naċ ḃfuil mise
'Gus mo ṁúirnín bán
I g-cúige Laiġean
No i g-condaé an Chláir.

Mo ḃrón naċ ḃfuil mise
'Gus mo ṁíle gráḋ
Air bord loinge
Triall go 'Meiricá.

Leabuiḋ luaċra
Ḃí fúm aréir,
Agus ċaiṫ mé amaċ é
Le teas an laé.

Táinig mo ġráḋ-sa
Le mo ṫaeḃ
Guala air ġualain
Agus beul air beul.

Ḃeurfaiḋ mé ann so abrán gráḋ eile, an t-abrán an-ċliúṫaċ ainmneaṁuil sin, an Droiġneán Donn, mar fuaras é dá ḃliaḋain deug ó soin o ṡean-ṡear, Ḃáiteur Sgurrlóg, i gcondaé Roscomáin, fear do fuair bás o ṡoin. Ḃeirim ann so é, mar tá sé rud-beag eugsaṁuil ó'n g-cóip do ṫug Miss Brúc agus ó'n g-cóip do ṫug O h-Argadáin ná O Dálaiġ dúinn ; agus má éiriġeann sgoláire suas ariaṁ le cur i g-cló príoṁ-abrán na h-Éireann (agus is díob-san an Droiġneán Donn) i g-cuma ceart le stuideáraċt cúramaiġ orra, ní fuláir* dó an oiread cóip eugsaṁuil do ḃeiṫ aige agus is féidir leis ḟáġail. Ní'l an ċóip seó ró ċosṁúil le aon ċeann eile air a ḃfuil fios agam-sa, agus tá diċfir mór idir í agus an t-abrán i leaḃar an h-Argadánaiġ.

An Droiġneán Donn.

Saoileann ceud fear gur leó féin mé nuair ólaim lionn,
'S téiḋeann dá dtrian síos díom nuair smaoiniġim air do ċómráḋ liom.
Do ċum is míne 'ná an síoda air Ṡliaḃ Ui Ḟloinn,
'S go ḃfuil mo ġráḋ-sa mar ḃláṫ an áirne air an droiġneán donn.

* Deir siad i g Connaċtaiḃ "ní ṁór dó," i. is éigin dó.

My grief, and my trouble!
  Would he and I were
In the province of Leinster,
  Or county of Clare.

Were I and my darling—
  Oh, heart-bitter wound!—
On board of the ship
  For America bound.

On a green bed of rushes
  All last night I lay,
And I flung it abroad
  With the heat of the day.

And my love came behind me—
  He came from the South;
His breast to my bosom,
  His mouth to my mouth.

I shall here give another love song, that very renowned and famous one, "The Drinaun Dunn" (Brown Blackthorn), as I got it twelve years ago from an old man, one Walter Sherlock, in the County Roscommon, a man who is since dead. I give it here as it is slightly different from the copies which Miss Brooke, Hardiman, and O'Daly give, and if any scholar ever rises up to print the prime songs of Erin—and "The Drinaun Dunn" is one of them—in right form, and making a careful study of them, he would want to have as many different versions as he can get. This copy is not very like any other one that I know, and there is great difference between it and the song as given in Hardiman's Book.

THE DRINAUN DUNN (BROWN BLACKTHORN).

A hundred men think that I am their own, when I drink ale (with them),
But two-thirds of them go down (*i.e.* retire) from me, when I think of your conversation with me;
Your form smoother than the silk that is on the mountain of O'Flynn,
And sure my love is like the blossom of the sloe on the brown blackthorn.

Agus slán feasta do'n ḃaile údaiġ,* ṡiar ameasg na g-crann
Is ann sin atá mo ṫarraingt go luaṫ 'gus go mall,
'S iomḋa anaċ fliuċ salaċ agus bóiṫrín cam.
Gaḃail idir mé 's an baile ḃfuil mo stóirín ann.

Tá píbín ó mo ċeud-searc ann mo ṗóca síos,
Agus fir Éireann ní leiġeasfadaois mo ḃrón, faraor!
Tá mé réiḋ leat go ndeuntar dam cóṁra ċaol
'S go ḃfásfaiḋ an feur 'nn a ḋiaiġ sin tríd mo lár aníos.

'S a Ṗaidiḋ a.. misde leat mé ḃeiṫ tinn
No a Ṗaidiḋ an misde leat mé dul 'sa 'g cill?
A Ṗaidiḋ an ċúil ċeangailte 's é do ḃeul atá binn,
'S go dtéidim 'san dtalaṁ béiḋ mo ġean ort faoi do ċóṁráḋ liom.

Is fear gan ċéill a raċfaḋ a' dréim leis an gcloiḋe ḃeiḋ' árd
'S cloiḋe íseall le na ṫaoiḃ air a leagfaḋ sé a láṁ.
Ciḋ gur árd é an crann caorṫainn bíonn sé searḃ ar a ḃárr
'S fásann sméarṫa 'gus suġ-craeḃa air an g-crann is ísle bláṫ.

'S a Ṁuire ḋílis créad deunfas mé má imṫiġeann tu uaim,
ní'l eólas ċum do ṫiġe agam, ċum d'agaird ná do ċruaċ,
Cóṁairle ḋíleas do ṫug mo ṁuinntir ḋam gan eulóġ leat,
'S go raiḃ ceud cor ann do ċroiḋe-stiġ 'gus na míle cleas.

Is fíor-ċaoin milis an dán so, agus ní'l áit air biṫ de 'n tír naċ ḃfuil sé le fáġail fós, agus tá sé ċoṁ coitċionn i m Beurla a's atá se i nGaeḋeilg, aċt ní ḃfáġmaoid i g-cóṁnuiḋe na ḃéarsaiḋ ceudna ann. Ḃí sean-ḃean ann do ġaḃaḋ ḋam é a ḃfad ó ṡoin, agus níor táinig sí ariaṁ do'n ċeáṫaṁain sin

"Ciḋ gur árd é an crann caorṫainn," naċ silead na déoir as a súil. Ag so abrán beag simpliḋe eile do fuair mé ó ṡean ṗíobaire dar b' ainm Grín i g-Condaé Ros-comáin.

*="úd," i gConnaċtaiḃ.

And farewell henceforth to yon town, westward amongst the trees,
It is there that my drawing is, early and late;
Many is the wet dirty morass and crooked road
Going between me and the town in which my treasureen is.

There is a ribbon from my first love in my pocket below,
And the men of Erin, they could not cure my grief, alas!
I am done with you, until a narrow coffin be made for me,
And till the grass shall grow, after that, up through my middle.

And, Oh, Paddy, do you think the worse of it (are you sorry), me to be ill?
Or, Oh, Paddy, do you think the worse of it, me to go into the churchyard?
Oh, Paddy of the bound back hair, it is your mouth is sweet,
And until I go into the ground my affection will be on you for your conversation with me.

He is a man without sense would go contend with a ditch that would be high,
And a low ditch by his side on which he might lay his hand (to vault across);
Although it is high, the rowan-berry tree, it bees* bitter out of the top,
While blackberries and raspberries grow on the tree that is lowest of blossom.

And, Oh, dear Mary (Virgin), what shall I if you go from me?
I have no knowledge (of how to go) to your house, your haggard, or your stacks;
A faithful counsel my people gave me not to elope with you,
For that there were a hundred twists in your heart, and the thousands of tricks.

This poem is truly gentle and sweet, and there is no spot in the country where it is not to be still found, and it is as common in English as it is in Irish, but we do not always find in it the same verses. There was an old woman in it, long ago, who used to sing it to me, and she never came to this verse—

Although the rowan-berry tree is high, etc.,

that she used not to shed tears from her eye. Here is another little simple song that I got from an old piper, named Green, in the county Roscommon.

---

* Usual Anglo-Irish for "it always is," or "it does be."

IS TRUAĠ GAN MISE I SACSANA.

Is truaġ gan mise i Sacsana
  I bFrainc ná 'sa' Spáin
Ná ṫall annsna siar-Indeaċaiḃ
  Mar a g-cóṁnuiġeann mo ġráḋ bán.
Agus Máire an ċúil ḋualaiġ
  'Nna suiḋe idir mo ḋá láiṁ,
A's go mbéiḋinn-se 'gá breugaḋ
  Go h-éiriġe an lá* báin.

Nuair luiḋim air mo leabaiḋ
  Ní'l sóċaṁuil le fáġail,
'S go bfuil arraing ann mo ṫaoiḃ ḋeas
  Agus loit sí mo lár.
Doċtúiriḋe na cruinne
  'S iad uile le fáġail,
Ní'l mo leiġeas ag an méad sin
  Aċt ag Máire an ċúil ḃáin.

Is fada mé ag imṫeaċt
  Air ṫuarasg mná tiġe,
A macsaṁuil ní ḟacaiḃ mise
  I mbaile no i dtír.
Dá bfeicfeá-sa an stuaiḋ-bean
  Air ṫaoiḃ Ċnuic-na-siḋe,
Dual d'á gruaig ḃáin
  'S é 'dá fuadaċ le gaoiṫ.

Ní'l aon abrán is simpliḋe ann san leaḃar so 'ná an ceann so. Ní'l sé cosṁúil le h-obair fir do ċleaċtaḋ dánta do ḋeunaṁ, agus is cosṁúile le h-abrán beurla é 'ná le h-abrán gaeḋeilg, óir ní'l an ċoṁ-ḟuaim ċéadna i ndó no i dtrí focalaiḃ anns gaċ líne, mar atá annsna sean-abránaiḃ eile; ní'l coṁ-ḟuaim ann san abrán so aċt aṁáin i ndeire an dara líne agus an ċeaṫraṁaḋ líne,—rud ċruṫuiġeas naċ bfuil sé an sean, agus naċ obair báird aċt obair duine-tíre éigin é.

---

* "Lá"="Lae," ann so.

I WISH I WERE IN ENGLAND.

Pity I am not (*i.e.*, I wish I were) in England,
In France, or in Spain,
Or over in the West Indies,
Where my white love lives,
And Mary of the tressy *cool*
Sitting between my two hands,
And sure I would be coaxing her,
Until the rise of the white day.

When I lie upon my bed,
There is no relief to be got,
And sure there is a stitch in my right side,
And she has wounded my middle.
The doctors of the universe,
And they all to be got—
My curing is not with all that number,
But with Mary of the fair *cool*.

It is long I am going
In search of a woman-of-the-house,
And image of her I never saw
In town or in country.
If you were to see the lovely lady
On the side of the Fairy's Hill,
A tress of her fair hair,
And it being violently-forced with the wind.

There is no song in this book more simple than this. It is not like the work of a man who used to practise making poems, and it is more like an English song than an Irish one, for there is not the same co-sound (vowel rhyme) in two or three words in each line as there is in the other old songs; there is no vowel rhyme in this song except at the end of the second and fourth lines, a thing which proves that it cannot be very old, and, that it is not the work of a bard, but of some peasant.

Sí seó an áit dam aḃráinín beag de'n tsórt ceudna do ċur síos. Ḃean éigin do ṫug gráḋ do ṫáilliúr do rinne é. Fuair mise ó ṡean-ḟear, Ḃáitéar Sgurrlóg, i g-condaé Roscomáin é, aċt tá an fear o a ḃfuair mé oċt mbliaḋna ó ṡoin é marḃ anois. Tá sé an-tsimpliḋe, agus gaċ uile focal d'á ndubairt mé i dtaoiḃ an aḃráin deirionnaiġ is fíor é i dtaoiḃ an aḃráin seó mar an g-ceudna.

TÁILLIÚIRÍN AN EUDAIĠ.

Fágfaiḋ mé an baile seó
Mar tá sé gránna,
Agus raċfaiḋ mé mo ċóṁnuiḋe
Go Claiḋ-Ui-Ġeaḋra.
An áit a ḃfuiġfead póga
'Óm' stóirín agus ceud fáilte,
'Óm' ḃog ċalamáinín (?) bó (?)*
Agus pósfad leis an táilliúr.

A ṫáilliúir, a ṫáilliúir
'S a ṫáilliúirín an éudaiġ,
Ní deise liom mar ġearras tu
'Ná mar ċumas tu na bre 'ga,
Ni truime liom bró ṁuilinn
'S í tuitim i loc Éirne,
'Ná gráḋ buan an táilliúir
Tá i mbrollaċ mo léine.

Shaoil mise féin
Mar do ḃí mé gan eólas
Go mbainfinn liom do láṁ
No fáinne an ṗósta,
Agus ṡaoil mé 'nna ḋiaiġ
Go mbuḋ tu an reult-eólais,
No bláṫ na sug-craoḃ
Air gaċ taoiḃ de na bóiṫrín'.

---

* Ḃ 'éidir=óm' ḃog ċolamáinín (=colum óig).

This is the place to put down another little song of the same sort. It was some woman who gave love to a tailor who made it. I got it from an old man, Walter Sherlock, in the County Roscommon, but the man from whom I got it eight years ago is now dead. It is very simple, and every word I said about the last song is true of this one also.

THE TAILOREEN OF THE CLOTH.

I will leave this village
Because it is ugly,
And I go to live
At Cly-O'Gara?
The place where I will get kisses
From my treasureen, and a *Céad fáilte*
From my soft, young little dove,
And I shall marry the tailor.

Oh, tailor, oh, tailor,
Oh, tailor*een* of the cloth,
I do not think it prettier how you cut (your cloth)
Than hov you shape the lies;
Not heavier would I think the quern of a mill,
And it falling into Loch Erne,
Than the lasting love of the tailor
That is in the breast of my shirt.

I thought, myself,
As I was without knowledge,
That I would seize your hand with me
Or the marriage ring,
And I thought after that
That you were the star of knowledge
Or the blossom of the raspberries
On each side of the *boreen* (little road)

Tá ceann de na ḃeursaiḃ seó le fáġail i n-abrán eile, agallaṁ no cóṁráḋ idir buaċaill óg do ḃí ag fágḃáil na h-Éireann agus mnaoi óig tá ag labairt leis. Deir sé léiṫi ann san g-ceud rann naċ bfuil dadaṁ aige aċt a ṡláinte aṁáin, agus deir sésin le greann óir is follasaċ go mb'ḟearr leis i d'imṫeaċt uaiḋ. Ni ċreideann sise é agus tosuiġeann sí ag claṁsán. Ag so é.

Tá cailín óg 'sa 'mbaile seó.

(An Buaċaill).

Tá cailín ann san mbaile seo
'S is ainm dí-se Máire,
Do ṫug mé gráḋ 'gus taiṫneaṁ dí
Tar cailínib na h-áite,
Ní'l ór agam, ní 'l airgead
Ná aon niḋ aċt mo ṡláinte,
'S má's roġa leat fear folaṁ
Biḋim agad agus fáilte.

(An Cailín).

A óganaiġ óig
A bfuil ór-buiḋe ann a ṗócaib
Go bfeiciḋ mé do h-allaiḋe
Geala, 'gus do ċóirtiḋe,
Go bfeiciḋ mé do ġáirdín
Lán de gaċ tóraḋ,*
Agus na ceudṫa ag fáġail báis
Le gráḋ do ṗórta.

Ṡaoil me féin
Mar bí mé gan eólas
Go mbeurfá ḋam do láṁ
No fáinne an ṗórta,
Agus ṡaoil mé 'nna ḋéiġ sin
Go mbuḋ tu an reult eólais
No bláṫ na súġ-ċraob
Air gaċ taoib de'n bóiṫrín.

* Recte "toraḋ," ni "tóraḋ."

One of these verses is to be found in another song, a dialogue or conversation between a young lad who was leaving Erin and a young woman who is speaking with him. He says to her in the first verse that he has nothing but his health, and he says that in sport, for it is evident that he would prefer her not to go away from him. She does not believe him, and begins to complain. Here it is :—

THERE'S A GIRL IN THIS TOWN.

(THE BOY).

There's a girl in this town,
    And her name it is Maurya,
I gave her love and liking
    Beyond all the girls of the place.
I have no gold, I have no silver,
    Nor anything but my health,
And if an empty man is your choice
    You may have me and welcome.

(THE GIRL).

O young youth,
    In whose pockets is the yellow gold,
That I may see your halls
    Bright, and your coaches,
That I may see your garden
    Full of every fruit,
And the hundreds dying
    For love of your marrying.

I thought, myself,
    For I was without knowledge,
That you would give me your hand
    Or the wedding-ring,
And I thought after that
    That you were the star of knowledge,
Or the blossom of the strawberry
    On each side of the boreen.

(An Buaċaill).

Is buaċaillín boċt mé
Ag fágbáil na h-Éireann
Ag imṫeaċt ċum na Fraince
I n-airm Ríġ Seumais,
Ḋíol mé mo ḋúiṫċe
Air ċárta diġe géire,
'S a bean an tiġe na páirte
Taḃair fliuċaḋ mo ḃéil dam.

(An Cailín).

A ógánaiġ óig
Ḃfuil an t-ór buiḋe ann a ṗéarlaiḃ
Agus an iomarcuiḋ ban óg
Ag pógaḋ do ḃéilín,
Nár ḟágaiḋ mise an saoġal so
Tá biodánaċ breugaċ
Go n-oilfiḋ mé do leanabán
Air ḃrollaċ geal mo léine.

Tá píosa binn eile ann a ḃfáġmaoid an ráḋ ceudna, "Reult an eólais" agus is aoiḃinn an ráḋ é. Is ag cur i g-céill atá sé go mbíonn eólas dúbalta agus géir-inntinn meudaiġṫe go mór, ag an té atá i ngráḋ. Tá an gráḋ mar reult, agus tá sé mar reult-eólais mar ġeall ar an g-caoi ann a n-osglann sé ár g-ceud-faṫa, go mbiḋmíd dúbalta níos eudtroime níos beóḃa agus géire 'ná ḃíamar roiṁe sin. Tuigmíd ann sin glóir agus áilleaċt an tsaoġail i rioċt nár ṫuigeamar ariaṁ go dtí sin é. Ag só an píosa air ar labras, abrán naċ féidir a ḟáruġaḋ i dteanga ar biṫ ar a ṁillseaċt agus ar a ḟíor-ċaoine.

A Óġánaiġ an Ċúil Ċeangailte.

A óġánaiġ an ċúil ċeangailte
Le a raiḃ mé seal i n-éinfeaċt
Ċuaiḋ tu 'réir, an bealaċ so
'S ni ṫáinig tu do m'ḟeuċaint.
Ṡaoil mé naċ ndeunfaiḋe doċar duit
Dá dtiucfá, a's mé d' iarraiḋ,
'S gur b'í do ṗóigín ṫaḃairfeaḋ sólás
Dá mbeiḋinn i lár an ḟiaḃrais.

(THE BOY).

I am a poor bohaleen
A-leaving Ireland,
Going into France
In the army of King James.
I sold my estate
For a quart of sour drink,
And, O woman of the house, of the part (*i.e.*, of my love)
Give me the wetting of my mouth (*i.e.*, a drink).

(THE GIRL).

O young youth,
Who has the yellow gold in his pearls,
And too many young women
Kissing your small mouth,
That I may never leave this world
Which is slanderous and lying
Until I rear your children
On the white bosom of my shirt.

There is another melodious piece in which we find the same expression, "star of knowledge," and a lovely expression it is. It is making us understand it is, that there be's double knowledge and greatly increased sharp-sightedness to him who is in love. The love is like a star, and it is like a star of knowledge on account of the way in which it opens our senses, so that we be double more light, more lively and more sharp than we were before. We understand then the glory and the beauty of the world in a way we never understood it until that. Here is the piece of which I spoke, a song which cannot be surpassed in any language for its sweetness and true gentleness.

RINGLETED YOUTH OF MY LOVE.

Ringleted youth of my love,
With thy locks bound loosely behind thee,
You passed by the road above,
But you never came in to find me;
Where were the harm for you
If you came for a little to see me,
Your kiss is a wakening dew
Were I ever so ill or so dreamy.

Dá mbeiḋeaḋ maoin agam-sa
Agus airgead ann mo ṗóca
Ḋeunfainn bóiṫrín aiṫ-giorraċ
Go dorus tiġe mo stóirín,
Mar súil le Dia go g-cluinnfinn-se
Torann binn a ḃróige,
'S is fad an lá ann ar ċodail mé
Aċt ag súil le blas do ṗóige.

A's ṡaoil me a stóirín
Go mbuḋ gealaċ agus grian ṫu,
A's ṡaoil mé 'nna ḋiaiġ sin
Go mbuḋ sneaċta ar an tsliaḃ ṫu,
A's ṡaoil mé 'nn a ḋiaiġ sin
Go mbuḋ lóċrann o Ḋia ṫu,
No gur ab tu an reult-eólais
Ag dul rómam a's mo ḋiaiġ ṫu.

Ġeall tu sioda 's saitin dam
Callaiḋe* 's bróga árda,
A's ġeall tu tar éis sin
Go leanfá tríd an tsnáṁ mé.
Ni mar sin atá mé
Aċt mo sgeaċ i mbeul bearna,
Gaċ nóin a's gaċ maidin
Ag feuċaint tiġe m' aṫar.

Ag so abrán fír-ṁilis eile tá cosṁúil le píosa as Ċúige Muṁan tá sé ċoṁ binn sin, aċt creidim gur abrán Connaċtaċ é. Tá an ráḋ sin "reult an eólais" ann san bpíosa so mar an g-ceudna. Is follasaċ go bfuil sé briste suas go mór agus naċ bfuil an t-iomlán ann.

* sórt sgáile no cáis, creidim.

If I had golden store
I would make a nice little boreen
To lead straight up to his door,
The door of the house of my storeen;
Hoping to God not to miss
The sound of his footfall in it,
I have waited so long for his kiss
That for days I have slept not a minute.

I thought, O my love! you were so—
As the moon is, or sun on a fountain,
And I thought after that you were snow,
The cold snow on top of the mountain;
And I thought after that, you were more
Like God's lamp shining to find me,
Or the bright star of knowledge before,
And the star of knowledge behind me.

You promised me high-heeled shoes,
And satin and silk, my storeen,
And to follow me, never to lose,
Though the ocean were round us roaring;
Like a bush in a gap in a wall
I am now left lonely without thee,
And this house I grow dead of, is all
That I see around or about me.*

Here is another truly sweet song, which is like a piece out of Munster, it is so melodious, but I believe it is a Connacht song. The expression "star of knowledge" is in this piece also. It is evidently greatly broken up, and the whole not in it.

---

*Literally. O youth of the bound back hair, With whom I was once together. You went by this way last night, And you did not come to see me. I thought no harm would be done you If you were to come and to ask for me, And sure it is your little kiss would give comfort. If I were in the midst of a fever.

If I had wealth And silver in my pocket, I would make a handy boreen To the door of the house of my storeen; Hoping to God that I might hear The melodious sound of his shoe, And long (since) is the day on which I slept, But (ever), hoping for the taste of his kiss.

And I thought, my storeen, That you were the sun and the moon, And I thought after that, That you were snow on the mouutain, And I thought after that That you were a lamp from God, Or that you were the star of knowledge Going before me and after me.

An Ṁaiġdean Óg.

Dá mbeiḋ' áitreaḃ agam féin
No gaḃáltas a's réim
Caoiriġ breáġ' bána
Ar árd-ċnoc no sléiḃ,
Sláinte agus méin
Agus gráḋ ceart d'á réir
Ḃeiḋinn-se 's mo ġráḋ geal
Go sáiṁ ann san tsaéġal.

Tá maiġdean óg 'san tír
'S is réaltan eólais í,
Grian breáġ ar bórd í
A's toġa de na mnáiḃ*
A cum fada breáġ
'S a cúilín craṫaċ bán
S gaċ alt léi ar lúṫ-ċriṫ
O ḃúcla go bráġaid.

Dá mbeiḋinn-se 's mo rún
Ar ċoill ag buain cnó
No ar [ṫaoiḃ] lisín aoiḃinn
'S gan dídionn orrainn aċt ceó,
Ḃeiḋeaḋ mo ċroiḋe-se d'á ḃreóġaḋ
Le díogras d'á póig
'S gur b'é gráḋ ceart do ċlaoiḋ mé
'S do ḟíor-sgaip mo ṡnóḋ.

Dá mbéiḋinn-se 's mo ġráḋ
Ar ṫaoiḃ ċnuic no báin
'S gan feóirling ann ár bróca
Ná lón ċum na sliġe,
Ḃeiḋ' mo ṡúil-se le Críost
Le ár ndóċaint† gan ṁoill
A's go dtógfaiḋ mo stór geal
An brón so de m' ċroiḋe.

---

* "Toġa gaċ óigḟir í," san MS., aċt tá rud éigin amúġa 'san ḃeurla so.

† "Go ḃráġmaois ár ndoċain gan ṁoill" san MS.

THE YOUNG MAIDEN.

If I had a dwelling to myself,
Or a holding and position,
    Fine white sheep
On high hill or mountain,
Health and beauty,
And right love accordingly,
    I and my bright love would be
Quietly off in the world.

There is a young maiden in the land,
And she is a star of knowledge,
    A splendid sun at table she is,
And a choice one of women ;
Her form long and fine,
Her cooleen shaking, fair,
    And every joint with her in an agile-quivering
From her buckles to her neck.

If I and my secret love were to be
At the wood gathering nuts,
    Or on the side of a pleasant lis (rath or moat),
With no shelter over us but mist,
My heart would be pining
With affection for her kiss,
    And sure it was right love destroyed me,
And truly-scattered my complexion.

If I and my love were
On the side of a hill or a waste (?),
    Without a farthing in our pocket
Or provisions for the way,
My hope would be with Christ
That we would get plenty without delay,
    And that my bright treasure would lift
This grief off my heart.

Dá mbéiḋinn-se 's mo ġráḋ
Cois taoide no tráiġ
'S gan aon neaċ beó 'nn ár dtimċioll
An oiḋċe fada, 's lá;
Do ḃéiḋinn-se ag cóṁráḋ
Le Neiliḋ an ċúil ḃáin
Is liom-sa 'buḋ h-aoiḃinn
Ḃeiṫ ag coiṁdeaċt mo ġráḋ.

Aċt ní ṁeasaim go ḃfuil aon aḃrán gráḋ níos leaṫnuiġṫe ar fud na tíre agus níos coitċionna i mbeul na sean daoine 'ná an dán do rinne Tomás Láidir Coisdeala (no Coisdealḃaċ mar atá an t-ainm sgrioḃṫa go minic) os cionn an ċailín ṁí-áġaṁuil sgiaṁaiġ .i. Úna nic Ḋiarmada d'á dtug sé gráḋ. Ní raiḃ aon fear i n-Éirinn le na linn buḋ ṁó neart agus lúṫ 'ná an Tomás so, agus sin é an fáṫ faoi a ḃfuair sé a leas-ainm, Tomás Láidir. Ní ḃíḋeaḋ na seanċuiḋe ariaṁ tuirseaċ ag innsint sgeul iongantaċ d'á ṫaoiḃ. Ṁair sé i n-aimsir an Dara Searluis, saoilim, agus ḃí a lán talṁan ag a ṁuinntir, aċt tar éis Cromuil do ṫeaċt go h-Éirinn ċaill se an ċuid buḋ ṁó ḋí, agus ṫáinig sí i seilḃ na nDíolún i g-condaé Sligiġ agus i g-condaé Ṁuiġ-eó. Do ḃí an Tomás Láidir ċoṁ luaṫ sin go mbeurfaḋ sé ar ḃromaċ trí ḃliadain, naċ raiḃ srian air ariaṁ, agus ḃí sé ċoṁ láidir sin go g-congṁóċaḋ sé é gan leigean dó imṫeaċt ċoṁ minic agus ḃéarfaḋ sé greim ar a ṁuing. Deir siad gur ḃ'é seó an ċeud ġníoṁ mór do rinne sé. Nuair ḃí sé 'nna ḃuaċaill ag fás, timċioll seaċt mbliaḋna deug d'aois, ṫáinig gaisgiḋeaċ go dtí an baile-mór Sligeaċ, agus ċuir se dubḟlán faoi an tír ar fad, ag iarraiḋ fir a raċfaḋ ag coruiġeaċt no ag spáirn leis. 'S é an gnáṫas do ḃí aca an t-am sin, gur ḃ'éigin do'n ċáṫair ann a dtiucfaḋ gaisgiḋeaċ de'n tsórt sin an gaisgiḋeaċ sin ċoṫuġaḋ agus ṫógḃáil no go ḃfuiġfeaḋ siad fear eile a ḃuailfeaḋ é ag coruiġeaċt.

Ṫáinig an lá ann ar ċruinniġ an condaé uile go Sligeaċ le feicsint an raiḃ aon duine a raċfaḋ ag coruiġeaċt leis'an ngaisgiḋeaċ, agus ḃí dearḃráṫair aṫar an Ċoisdealaiġ ag dul ann mar an g-ceudna. D' iarr Tomás air leigean dó dul leis, agus tar éis impiḋe fada ṫug sé cead dó. Nuair ṫángadar go Sligeaċ ḃí na sluaiġte ann rompa, agus ċuaiḋ siad amaċ air an ḃfaiṫċe no ar an moinfeur 'n áit a raiḃ an gaisgiḋeaċ. Gaċ uile ḋuine do ḃí dul ag coruiġeaċt leis, ḃíḋeaḋ sé d'á leagaḋ, agus d'á ċaṫaḋ ar an talaṁ, agus ní raiḃ fear air biṫ ionnánn seasaṁ 'nna aġaiḋ. Connairc colceaṫair an Ċoisdealaiġ óig Tomás ag craṫaḋ agus

If I and my love were
Beside the tide or the shore
    Without anyone alive around us,
And the long night and the day
I would be conversing
With Nelly of the fair cool,
    It's I who would think it pleasant
To be accompanying my love.

But I do not think that there is any love song more widely spread throughout the country and more common in the mouth of the people than the poem which Tumaus Loidher (strong Thomas) Cosdello, or Coisdealbhach (foot-shaped ?), as the name is often written, composed over the unfortunate and handsome girl Una MacDermott, to whom he had given love. There was no man in Ireland in his time of greater strength and activity than this Tumaus, and that was why he got his nick-name of Tumaus Loidher. The Shanachies used never to be tired of telling wonderful stories about him. He lived in the time of Charles II, I think, and his people had much land, but after Cromwell's coming to Ireland they lost the greater portion of it, and it came into the possession of the Dillons in the counties Sligo and Mayo. This Tumaus Loidher was that quick that he would overtake a three-year-old colt that never had been bridled, and he was that strong that as often as ever he got a hold of his mane he would hold him, without allowing him to get away. They say that this was the first great deed that he performed: When he was a boy growing up, about seventeen years of age, there came a champion or bully to the town of Sligo, and he put a challenge under (*i.e.* challenged) the whole county, looking for a man who would go to wrestle or contend with him. The custom which they had at that time was, that the city into which a champion of this sort would come, was obliged to support and maintain the champion until they could find another man who would beat him at wrestling.

The day came when the whole county gathered together to Sligo to see was there any man who would go wrestling with the champion, and Costello's father's brother was going there likewise. Tumaus asked him to allow him to go with him, and after long entreaty he gave him leave. When they came to Sligo there were multitudes there before them, and they went out on the lawn or meadow where the champion was. Everyone who was going wrestling with him he used to be throwing him and hurling him on the ground, and there was no man able to stand before him. Young Costello's uncle saw

air bruiṫ. "Cad tá ort?" ar sé. "Óra," ar sé, "leig dam, leig dam, dul ag coruiġeaċt leisean." "A amadáin ṁóir," arsa an colceaṫair leis, "cad é sin tá tu ráḋ? an maiṫ leat go marḃóċaḋ an gaisgiḋeaċ ṫu." ? "Ní ṁarḃóċaiḋ sé mé," arsa an buaċaill, "is láidre mise 'ná eisean." "Leig dam do riġṫeaċa láiṁsiuġaḋ," arsa an sean-ḟear. Ṡín Tomás amaċ iad agus bí na féiṫeaċa bí ionnta ċoṁ teann agus ċoṁ cruaiḋ le iarann. Bhí an buaċaill ag cur impiḋe air an t-sean-ḟear agus ag síor-iarraiḋ cead air, go raiḃ se sáruiġṫe faoi ḋeire agus ṫug sé cead dó dul ag troid leis an ngaisgiḋeaċ. Ní raiḃ aon ḟear eile ag teaċt an t-am sin, óir ḃí siad uile buailte ag an ngaisgiḋeaċ an méad do ċuaiḋ ag coruiġeaċt leis, agus ḃí faitċios air na daoiniḃ uile. Ṡeas amaċ an Coisdealaċ ann sin agus duḃairt sé, "raċfaiḋ mise ag spáirn leat." Rinne an gaisgiḋeaċ gáire nuair ċonnairc sé an garsún óg dul amaċ leis agus duḃairt sé, "má tá tu críona a ġarsúir big," ar sé, "fanfaiḋ tu mar a ḃfuil tu; agus ni ṫiucfaiḋ tu ag troid liom-sa." "Deunfaiḋ mé mo ḋiċċioll leat, ar ṁóḋ ar biṫ," ar Tomás.

Is aṁlaiḋ bud ġnáṫ leó coruiġeaċt do ḋeunaṁ an tráṫ sin, crios no beilt leaṫair do ċeangailt timċioll cuim an dá ḟear, agus greim do ṫaḃairt do gaċ ḟear ar ċrios an ḟir eile, agus nuair beiḋeaḋ siad réiḋ agus nuair ḃéarfaiḋe an focal dóiḃ, ṫosóċaḋ siad ag coruiġeaċt. Nuair ċonnairc an sluaġ mór do ḃí cruinniġṫe ann sin an crios ag dul air Ṫomás óg do ġlaoḋ siad amaċ gan leigean dó dul ag troid, óir ḃí faitċios orra go marḃfaiḋe é, mar do ṁarḃ an gaisgiḋeaċ so cuid ṁaiṫ daoine roiṁe sin, agus ṡaoil siad uile naċ raiḃ cosṁúileaċt ar biṫ go dtiúḃraḋ buaċaill bog óg mar Tomás a anam uaiḋ. Aċt níor ṁaiṫ le Tomás éisteaċt leó, mar ṁoṫuiġ sé féin go raiḃ sé níos láidre 'ná ṡaoil na daoine. Ḃí an sean-ċolceaṫair ag seilt deór nuair ċonnairc sé naċ raiḃ aon ṁaiṫ ḋó beiṫ ag caint leis.

Ċuaiḋ an crios leaṫair air ann sin, agus fuair an gaisgiḋeaċ greim daingean air, agus fuair seisean greim maiṫ air ċrios a náṁaid. Tugaḋ orduġaḋ ḋóiḃ ann sin do ṫosuġaḋ ar a ċéile. Nuair fuair sé an focal ṫarraing Tomás a ḋá láiṁ do ḃí greamuiġṫe i mbeilt a náṁaid, asteaċ ċuige féin go h-obann, aċt níor ċuir an gaisgiḋeaċ cor as féin. Fuair Tomás bárróg air agus ṫug se an dara sásġaḋ ḋó aċt níor ċorruiġ an náṁad. "A ċolceaṫair ḋílis," ar Tomás, "cad tá ar an ḃfear so naċ ḃfuil sé ag coruiġeaċt liom, sgaoil díom é go ḃfeicfimid."

Tumaus quivering and boiling. "What's on you?" (What's the matter with you?) says he. "Ora," says he, "let me go to wrestle with him." "You great fool," says the uncle to him, "what's that you're saying? Do you want the champion to kill you?" "He won't kill me," says the lad; "I am stronger than he." "Let me feel your arms," says the old man. Tumaus stretched them out, and the muscles that were in them were as firm and hard as iron. The lad was beseeching the old man, and asking permission of him until he was tired at last, and gave him permission to go fight with the champion. There was no other man coming forward at this time, for the champion had beaten them all, as many as went wrestling with him, and the other people were afraid. Costello stood out then and said, "I'll go wrestling with you." The champion laughed when he saw the young gossoon going out against him, and he said, "If you're wise, little gossoon, you will stay where you are, and you won't come fighting with me." "I'll do my best with you, anyhow," says Tumaus.

Now this was the way it was customary with them to make a wrestling at this time; that was, to bind a girdle or belt of leather round about the body of the two men, and to give each man of them a hold on the other man's belt, and when they would be ready and the word would be given them they would begin wrestling. When the great multitude saw the belt going on young Tumaus, they cried out not to let him go fight, for they were afraid he would be killed, for this champion killed a good many people before that, and they thought there was no likelihood that a soft young boy like Tumaus would bring his life away from him; but Tumaus would not listen to them, for he felt himself that he was stronger than the people thought. The old uncle was shedding tears when he saw that it was no good for him to be talking to him.

The leather belt went on him then, and the champion got a firm hold of it, and he got a good hold of his enemy's belt. The order was then given them to begin on one another. When he got the word Tumaus suddenly drew in his two hands that were fastened in his enemy's belt towards himself, but the champion never put a stir out of himself. Tumaus got a leverage on him and gave him the second squeeze, but the enemy did not stir. "Dear uncle," said Tumaus, "what's on this man that he is not wrestling with me; loose him from me till we see?" Then the people came

Ṫáinig na daoine suas ann sin agus sgaoileadar láṁa an ġais-giḋiġ de 'n ċrios ann a raiḃ siad greamuiġṫe, agus ar an mball do'ṫuit an fear siar, agus é fuar marḃ,—ḃí cnáṁ a ḋroma briste leis an g-ceud ḟásgaḋ ṫug Tomás dó.

B'é sin an ċeud-ġaisgiḋeaċt do rinne Tomás ariaṁ, agus ṫuig sé féin ann sin go raiḃ sé níos láidre 'ná daoine eile. Chuir goḃa geall leis aon uair aṁáin go ndeunfaḋ sé ceiṫre crúḋa capaill naċ ḃfeudfaḋ sé a lúbaḋ ná a ndíriúġaḋ, aċt go g-caiṫfeaḋ sé na ceiṫre crúḋa cur le ċéile nuair a ḃeiḋeaḋ sé ag iarraiḋ a lúbaḋ. Créad do rinne an goḃa aċt cruaiḋe do ċur ionnta i n-áit iarainn. Ṫáinig Tomás agus ġlac sé na crúḋa ann a láiṁ agus ṫug sé fásgaḋ ḋóiḃ, aċt níor ċorruiġ sé iad, ṫug sé an dara fásgaḋ ḋóiḃ, aċt ní raiḃ maiṫ aige ann. "Dar mo láiṁ is maiṫ do rinne tu iad," ar sé, "caiṫfiḋ mé an cóta mór baint díom." Ḃain sé an cóta mór dé, agus ṫug sé an tríoṁaḋ teannaḋ ḋóiḃ, agus níor ḟeud sé a lúbaḋ, mar is cruaiḋe do ḃí ionnta, aċt rinne se greamanna díoḃ ann a ḋá láiṁ, aṁuil agus mar buḋ ġlaine iad. Ḃí an goḃa 'nna ḟeasaṁ ag an doras, mar ḃí faitċios air go mbrisfeaḋ na crúḋa, ciḋ gur dar leis féin buḋ rud do-ḋeunta é, agus ċoṁ luaṫ agus ċonnairc sé 'ḋá mbriseaḋ iad, amaċ leis, agus ṫarraing sé an doras 'nna ḋiaiġ. Ġlac lasaḋ feirge an Coisdealaċ nuair ċonnairc sé an cleas d'imir an goḃa air, agus ṫionntuiġ sé agus ċaiṫ se na píosaiḋ cruaiḋe do ḃí ann a láiṁ andiaiġ na goḃan, agus ṫeilg sé ċoṁ láidir sin iad gur ṫiomáin sé mar ṗeiléaraiḃ iad amaċ tríd an doras.

Tá an oiread sgeul ag na sean daoiniḃ air eaċtraiḃ agus gníoṁarṫaiḃ Ṫomáis Láidir (no ḃí cúig bliaḋna deug ó ṡoin) naċ sgurfainn go bráṫ d'á n-innsint dá dtosóċainn orra agus dá ḃ-feudfainn a n-innsint mar do ċualas iad, agus ar an áḋḃar sin ní innseóċaiḋ mé ann so aċt an ocáid faoi a ndearnaiġ sé an dán atá me dul d'á ṫaḃairt air Úna Nic Diarmada.

Ṫug Úna gráḋ ḋó-san, agus ṫug seisean gráḋ d' Úna. Ní raiḃ an Coisdealaċ saiḋḃir, aċt ḃí mórán maoine agus talṁan ag Mac Diarmada, agus d'orduiġ sé do'n inġin, Úna, gan ḃeiṫ ag caint ná ag cóṁráḋ le Tomás Láidir mar naċ leigfeaḋ sé ḋí a ṗósaḋ go bráṫ. Ḃí fear eile ann buḋ ḟaiḋḃre 'ná an Coisdealaċ, agus buḋ ṁian leis go bpósfaḋ sise an fear so. Nuair ḟaoil sé faoi ḋeire go raiḃ toil a inġine briste agus lúbṫa go leór aige, rinne sé fleaḋ no feusta mór agus ċuir sé cuireaḋ air ḋaoiniḃ-

up and they loosed the hands of the champion from the belt where they were fastened, and on the spot the man fell back, and he cold dead; his back-bone had been broken with the first squeeze that Tumaus gave him.

That was the first hero-feat that Tumaus ever performed, and he himself understood then that he was stronger than other people. A smith bet with him one day that he would make four horse-shoes which he would neither bend nor straighten, but that he must put the four shoes together when trying to bend them. What did the smith do but put steel into them in place of iron. Tumaus came, and he took the shoes in his hand, and he gave them a squeeze; but he never stirred them. He gave them the second squeeze, but there was no good for him in it. "By my hand, then," says he, "it's well you made them. I must take off my cotamore (great coat) to it." He threw the cotamore off him and he gave them the third tightening, but he could not bend them, because it was steel was in it; however, he made pieces of them in his two hands as if they were glass. The smith was standing at the door, as he was afraid that the shoes might break, although it was an impossibility, as it seemed to him; but as soon as he saw them breaking, out with him, and he pulled the door after him. Then Costello took a flame of wrath when he saw the trick the smith played him, and he turned round and hurled the pieces of steel that were in his hand out after the smith, and he flung them with such strength that he drove them out like bullets through the door.

The old people have, or they had fifteen years ago, so many stories about the adventures and deeds of Tumaus Loidher, that were I to begin on them, and were I able to tell them as I heard them, I would never cease telling of them, and for that reason I shall only speak here of the occasion on which he composed the poem I am about to give on Una* MacDermott.

Una gave him love, and he gave love to Una. The Costello was not rich, but MacDermott had much riches and land, and he ordered his daughter Una not to be talking or conversing with Tumaus Loidher, because he never would allow her to marry him. There was another man in it who was richer than the Costello, and he desired that she should marry this man. When he thought, at last, that his daughter's will was sufficiently broken and bent by him, he made a great collation, or feast, and sent an invitation to the gentlemen of the whole

* Una is pronounced "Oona" not "Yewna" as so many people now call it. This beautiful native name is now seldom heard, but it is absurdly Anglicised "Wyny" in Roscommon, and in some places "Winny."

uaisle an ċondaé uile, agus bí Tomás Láidir 'nna measg. Nuair bí an dinéar críoċnuiġṫe ċosuiġ siad ag ól sláinteaḋ agus duḃairt Mac Diarmada le na inġin, "fear suas," ar sé, "agus ól sláinte ar an té sin is fearr leat ann san g-cuideaċta so," mar ṡaoil sé go n-ólfaḋ sí sláinte ar an ḃfear saiḋḃir sin do ḃí leagṫa amaċ aige mar ċéile ḋí.* Ġlac sise an gloine, agus ṡeas sí suas, agus d'ól sí deoċ ar Ṫomás Láidir Coisdeala. Nuair ċonnairc an t-aṫair í ag deunaṁ sin ṫáinig fearg air agus ḃuail sé buille boise ar a leiṫ-cinn. Bhí náire uirri-se, agus ṫáinig deóra ann a súilib, aċt bí sí ro áird-inntinneaċ le leigean do na daoinib ḟeicsint go raib sí ag gol faoi an mbuille ṫug an t-aṫair dí, agus ṫóg sí borsa snaoisín agus ċuir sí sguibín dé 'nna sróin, ag leigean uirri gur b' é an snaoisin láidir do ḃain na deóra ḋí. D'ḟág Tomás Láidir an seomra ar an móimid. Is i dtaoib an niḋ a ṫárla ann sin a duḃairt sé an rann so ameasg móráin eile.

Naċ lágaċ a duḃairt páirte na ngeal-ċíoċ é,
Ag fásgaḋ a dá láiṁ 's ag miniuġaḋ a méar,
Ag cur sgáṫ air an áḋḃar agus í i bpéin,
A's cnead craiḋte air! buḋ láidir an snaoisín é.

Buaileaḋ Úna 'nic Diarmada tinn 'nna ḋiaiġ sin, leis an ngráḋ do ṫug sí ḋó, agus ni ráiḃ sí ag fáġail bisiġ ar biṫ ná leiġis ó aon rud, agus bí sí ċoṁ dona sin faoi ḋeireaḋ nár ḟeud sí a leabaiḋ d'ḟágḃáil. Ann sin agus ní go dtí sin, ṫug Mac Diarmada cead dí an Coisdealaċ do ġlaoḋaċ ċuici féin. Chuir Úna fios air agus ṫáinig sé, agus ṫreóruiġ siad go dtí seomra Úna é, agus ṫáinig a h-anam arís ċuici le sásúġaḋ inntinne nuair ċonnairc sí arís é. Rinne an lúṫġáire do ḃí uirri faoi n-a ḟeicsint an oireaḋ sin de ṁaiṫ ḋí, gur ṫuit sí faoi ḋeireaḋ ann a codlaḋ sáiṁ socair, an ċeud ċodlaḋ fuair sí le mìosaib, agus eisean 'nna ṡuiḋe cois na leapṫan agus ise ag congḃáil a láiṁe-sean ann a láiṁ-se féin. Suiḋ sé ann sin ar feaḋ tamaill ṁaiṫ, aċt mar naċ raiḃ sise ag dúisiúġaḋ agus mar bí leisg air beiṫ ag fanaṁaint ann sin, sgaoil sé a láṁ-san as a láiṁ-se, agus ċuaiḋ sé amaċ as an t-seomra agus síos na staiḋriḋe. Ní ḃfuair sé duine ar biṫ ann san teaċ, agus bí náire air d'ḟanaṁaint ann leis féin. Ġlaoḋ sé ar a ḟearḃróġanta dialaide do ċur ar na caplaib, agus do ḃeiṫ ag

* Feuċ an freagraḋ críona ṫug inġean eile nuair ċuir an t-aṫair an rud ceudna d'ḟiaċaib uirri, ann mo leaḃar Sgeuluiġeaċta, l. 153.

county, and Tumaus Loidher was among them. When the dinner was finished they began drinking healths, and MacDermott said to his daughter; "Stand up and drink the health of that person whom you like best in this company," because he thought she would drink the health of that wealthy man he had laid out for her as a consort.* She took the glass and stood up, and drank a drink on Tumaus Loidher Costello. When the father saw her doing that anger came upon him, and he struck her a blow of his palm on the side of the head. She was ashamed, and tears came into her eyes, but she was too high-spirited to let the people see that she was crying at the blow her father gave her, and she lifted a snuff-box and put a pinch of it to her nose, letting on that it was the strong snuff that knocked the tears out of her. Tumaus Loidher left the room upon the spot. It was anent the occurrence that happened there, that he spake this rann amongst many others—

Is it not courteously the child of the white breasts said it,
Wringing her two hands and smoothing her fingers,
Putting a shadow upon the reason, and she in pain,
And bitter destruction on it! it was a strong snuff.

After that Una MacDermott was stricken sick with the love she gave him, and she was getting no relief or cure at all from anything, and she was so bad at last that she was not able to leave her bed. Then, and not till then, MacDermott gave her leave to call to herself the Costello. Una sent for him, and he came, and they guided him to Una's chamber, and her soul came again to her with satisfaction of mind when she saw him. The joy that was on her at seeing him did her so much good that she at last fell into a pleasant quiet sleep, the first sleep she had got for months, and he sitting beside her bed, and she holding his hand in her own hand. He sat there for a good while, but as she was not awaking and as he was loath to be remaining there, he loosed his hand out of her hand, and went out of the room and down the stairs. He found nobody at all in the house, and he was ashamed to remain in it by himself. He called to his servant to saddle the horse and be going. He then got on his horse and rode slowly, slowly, from the house, thinking every moment that he would be sent for, and that they would ask him to return; accordingly, he

---

* See the clever answer of the girl who was desired by her father to do the same thing, in my Leabhar Sgeuluigheachta, p. 153.

imṫeaċt. Ċuaiḋ sé ar a ċapall ann sin, agus ṁarcáil sé go mall ó'n tiġ ag smuaineaḋ gaċ móimid go g-cuirfiḋe fios air, agus go n-iarrfaḋ siad air filleaḋ. D'ḟan sé mar sin, anaice leis an tiġ aċt ní raiḃ aon teaċtaire ag tíġeaċt le na ġlaoḋaċ ar ais. Ḃí a ṡearḃḟóġanta tuirseaċ ag fanaṁaint leis, agus b'ḟada leis an t-am a ḃí a ṁáiġistir ag marcuiġeaċt gan dul a ḃfad ó'n tiġ. Ṫosuiġ sé ag ráḋ le n-a ṁáiġistir naċ raiḃ muinntir Ṁic Ḋiar-mada, aċt ag magaḋ faoi, agus ċuir sé ann a ċeann é gur feall do ḃí siad ag deunaṁ air. Níor ċreid an Coistealaċ i dtosaċ gur ab' aṁluiḋ ḃí sé, aċt nuair naċ raiḃ duine ar biṫ ag teaċt ċuige agus nuair a ḃí an searḃḟóġanta ag síor-ċur an aṁarais seó ann a ċeann, do ṫosuiġ sé féin a ċreideaṁaint agus ṫug sé a ṁóid agus a ṁionna dar Dia agus Muire naċ dtion-ntóċaḋ sé ar ais go bráṫ agus naċ laiḃeóraḋ sé focal go deó le Úna no le muinntir Ḋiarmada muna nglaoḋfaiḋe ar ais é sul ċuaiḋ se ṫar aṫ na h-aiḃne bige, na Donóige. Nuair ċuaiḋ sé asteaċ 'san aḃain ní raċfaḋ sé ṫairsti, aċt d'ḟan sé 'san uisge ar feaḋ leaṫ-uaire agus níos mó, ag síor-ḟúil go dtiucfaḋ teaċtaire 'nna ḋiaiġ. Ṫosuiġ an searḃḟóġanta d'á cáineaḋ ann sin. "Is mór an t-iongnaḋ liom," ar sé, "duine uasal mar ṫusa do ḃeiṫ ag fuaraḋ 'san uisge seó air son mná ar biṫ ann san tsaoġal mór. Naċ beag d'uaiḃreas náire mar sin d'ḟulaing." "Is fíor ḋuit sin," ars an Coisdealaċ, agus ṫiomáin sé an capall suas ar an mbanca. Ar éigin ḃí sé ar an talaṁ tirm nuair ṫáinig teaċ-taire 'nna ḋiaiġ 'nn a lán-riṫ ó Úna, ag glaoḋaċ air do ṫeaċt ar ais ċuici go luaṫ. Aċt ní ḃrisfeaḋ an Coisdealaċ a ṁóid agus níor ḟill sé. Tar éis an Coisdealaċ d'imṫeaċt uaiṫi, níor ḋúisiġ Úna ar feaḋ tamaill áiḃḃeul-ṁóir. Ar ndúisiuġaḋ ḋí faoi ḋeireaḋ go h-aeraċ eudtrom b'é an ċeud rud do rinne sí fios do ċur ar an g-Coisdealaċ, aċt ḃí sé imṫiġṫe. Sgannruiġ si ann sin agus ċuir sí teaċtaire 'nn a ḋiaiġ, aċt níor ṫáinig an teaċtaire suas leis i n-am. Ġlac an Coisdealaċ lasaḋ-feirge ann sin agus ḃuail sé dorn ar an tsearḃḟóġanta do ṫug an droċ-ċóṁairle ḋó, gur ṁarḃ sé de'n ḃuille sin é.

Níor ḃfada 'nna ḋiaiġ sin gur ġoill an brón agus an cúṁa ċoṁ mór sin ar Úna gur ḟeirg sí, agus go ḃfuair sí bás. Níor ḟeud aon rud ḃí ar an doṁan sólas ar biṫ ṫaḃairt do'n Ċoisdealaċ 'nna ḋiaiġ sin. Ḃhí Úna curṫa ar oileáinín beag i lár Loċa Cé, agus ṫáinig an Coisdealaċ go bruaċ an loċa an oiḋċe 'réir a curṫa, agus ṡnáṁ sé amaċ go dti an oileán agus ċaiṫ sé é féin síos ar an uaiġ, agus ċuir sé an oiḋċe ṫairis ag faire agus ag gol

remained near the house, but there was no messenger coming to call him back. His servant was tired waiting for him to go on, and he thought it long the time that his master was riding without going far from the house. He began to say to his master that MacDermott's people were only humbugging him, and he put it into his head that they were doing an act of treachery on him. Costello did not at first believe that it was so, but when no one was coming to him, while the servant kept continually putting this suspicion into his head, he began, himself, to believe it, and took his vow and oath by God and Mary that he would never again turn back and never speak a word to Una or one of MacDermott's people unless he should be called back before he went across the ford of the little river, the Donogue. When he did go into the river he would not go across it, and he remained in the water for half an hour or more, ever hoping that a messenger might come after him. Then the servant began to revile him: "I think it a great wonder," he said, "for a gentleman like you to be cooling in this water for any woman at all in the great world; is it not small your pride, to endure a disgrace like that?" "That's true for you," said the Costello, and he drove his horse up upon the bank. Scarcely was he up on the dry ground when there came a messenger after him in a full run from Una, calling to him to come back to her quickly; but the Costello would not break his vow, and he did not return. After Costello's going from her, Una did not awake for an exceedingly long time. On awaking of her at last, airy and light, the first thing she did was to send for the Costello, but he was gone. She frightened at that, and sent a messenger after him, but the messenger did not come up with him in time. Costello took then a flame of anger and struck a fist upon the servant who gave him the bad advice, so that he killed him of that blow.

It was not long after this that grief and melancholy preyed so much upon Una that she withered away and found death. Nothing at all that was on the world could give any comfort to the Costello after that. Una was buried in a little island in the middle of Lough Cé, and Costello came to the brink of the lake the night after her burial and swam out to the island, and threw himself down upon her grave, and put the night past, watching and weeping over her

os a cionn. Rinne sé an rud ceudna an dara oiḋċe. Ṫáinig sé an tríoṁaḋ oiḋċe agus duḃairt sé os cionn na h-uaiġe mar ċualaiḋ mise é.

A Úna bán is gránna an luiḋe sin ort
Ar leabaiḋ caol árd ameasg na mílte corp
Muna dtagaiḋ tu fáiḋ* (?) orm a stáid-ḃean ḃí riaṁ gan loċt,
Ní ṫiucfaiḋ mé ċum na h-áite seó go bráṫ aċt aréir 's anoċt.

No mar fuair mé an ceaṫaṁa só i láiṁ-sgríḃinn ḋroċ-sgríoḃṫa, an t-aon ċeann amáin ann a ḃfuairear ariaṁ é,

A Úna bán is gránna an luiḋe sin ort
Air leabaiḋ caol árd, láiṁ leis na míltiḃ corp
Muna dtugaiḋ tu do láṁ dam a stáid-ḃean naċ ndearnaiḋ olc
ni ḟeuċfuiġear mo sgáile ar an tsráid seó ċoiḋċ' 'aċt anoċt.

Ní luaiṫe duḃairt sé sin 'ná ṁoṫuig sé Úna ag éiriġe suas agus ag bualaḋ boise éudroime ar a leiṫcinn, agus ċualaiḋ sé guṫ mar ġuṫ Úna ag ráḋ leis "na tarraiġ,"† agus d'imṫiġ sé go sásta ann sin gan filleaḋ go bráṫ.

Ḃí an ċuid eile de ḃeaṫa Ṫomáis láidir ċoṁ h-iongantaċ leis an sgeul so, agus do ḃiḋeaḋ an oiread sgeul ag na sean daoiniḃ i g-condaé Roscomáin agus i g-condaé Sligiġ d'á ṫaoiḃ agus cong-ḃóċaḋ duine ag éisteaċt leó air feaḋ oiḋċe iomláine aċt níor ċuimniġ mé iad uile nuair d'ḟeudfainn agus anois ni ṫig liom a ḃfáġail. Fuair sé bás faoi ḋeireaḋ. Ḃí fear de na Ruaḋánaiḃ agus ġeall na Díolúnaiġ duais dó dá marḃaḋ sé é. Agus sgaoil sé peiléar leis o ċúl cruaiċe móna agus ṁarḃ sé é. Ḃhí sé 'nna luiḋe ar feaḋ trí lá ar an talaṁ gan duine ar biṫ le na ṫógbáil mar ḃí faitċíos ar na daoiniḃ roiṁe. Mar ġeall ar an ngníoṁ sin ni leigfeaḋ na Coisdealaiġ do ṫáinig 'nna ḋiaiġ aon ḟear d'a'r ḃ'ainm Ruaḋán ḃeiṫ 'nna ċóṁnuiḋe ar a ndúiṫċe-sean. Aċt deir cuid eile gur ḃ'é a ḋearḃráṫair-sean Duḃáltaċ Caoċ do fuair bás mar so.

Ḃeurfaiḋ mé anois na ceaṫraṁna do rinne an Coisdealaċ ar Úna nic Ḋiarmada, mar ċualaiḋ mé iad o ṁórán daoine. Deir na daoine-tíre gur i g-"cruaḋ-ġaeḋeilge," atá siad, agus naċ

* "Fáiḋ," no "sáir," is é seó an focal ċualaiḋ mé ó gaċ uile ḋuine a raiḃ an rann so aige, agus iad a ḃfad ó ċéile, trí fiċe míle ó ċéile, aċt ni ṫuigim cad é an ċiall dé.

†=na tarr.

head. He did the same thing the second night; he came the third night and spake above her grave, as I heard it—

"O fair-haired Una, ugly is the lying that is upon you,
On a bed narrow and high among the thousand corpses,
If you do not come and give me a token (?), O stately woman, who was ever without a fault,
I shall not come to this place for ever, but last night and to-night."

Or, as I found this stanza in a very ill-written manuscript, the only one in which I ever did find it:

"Unless thou givest me thy hand, O stately woman who did no evil,
My shadow shall not be seen upon this street for ever but to-night."

No sooner did he say that than he felt Una rising up, and striking a light blow of her palm upon his cheek, and he heard a voice like Una's, saying, "Come not," and he then departed satisfied, without returning for ever.

The rest of the life of Tomaus Loidher was as wonderful as this story, and the old people in the Counties Roscommon and Sligo used to have as many stories about him as would keep a person listening to them for an entire night, but I did not collect them all when I was able, and now I cannot find them. He found death at last. There was a man of the Ruanes, and the Dillons promised him a reward if he would kill him, and he loosed a bullet at him from behind a turf clamp and killed him. He was lying for three days on the ground without any person to take him up, for they were afraid of him. On account of this deed the Costellos who came after him would not allow any man of the name of Ruane to live on their estate. But some say that it was his brother, Dooaltagh, or Dudley, the dim-eyed, who died in this manner.

I shall now give the stanzas which the Costello made about Una MacDermott as I heard them from many people. The country people say that they are in "cramp-Irish," and that there was never yet found a piper or a fiddler to play them on the pipes or the fiddle! There are a great many stanzas in the poem, but I never got the

fuaraḋ aon ṗíobaire ná aon ḃeilleadóir fós d'ḟeudfaḋ a seinnm ar a ṗíobaiḃ ná air a ḟidil! Tá a lán ceaṫrama ann san dán aċt ni ḃfuair mé an t-iomlán aca, ná an leaṫ. Ċualaiḋ mé na sgeulta so ar Ṫomás Láidir o Ṡeumas O h-Airt, ó Ḃáitéar Sgurlóg,—tá an ḃeirt aca marḃ anois—agus o Ṁártain O Ḃraonáin i g-condaé Roscomáin, aċt fuair mé cuid de na ceaṫramnaiḃ o ḟear i n-oileán Acaill, nár ċualaiḋ caint ariaṁ air Ṫomás Láidir.

Nuair fuair sé bás cuireaḋ é, mar d'orduiġ sé féin, ann san roilig agus ann san oileán ceudna ann ar cuireaḋ Úna, agus d'ḟás crann fuinnseóige as uaiġ Úna agus crann eile as uaiġ Ṫomáis, agus do ċlaon siad dá ċéile, agus níor sguireadar d'á ḃfás gur casaḋ agus gur lúbaḋ an dá ḃárr ar a ċeile i meaḋon na roilige, agus duḃairt daoine do ċonnairc iad, go raiḃ siad ann sin fós, aċt bí mise ar ḃruaċ Loċa Cé go déiġeanaċ agus níor ḟeud mé a ḃfeicsint, aċt ni raḃas ar an oileán.

ÚNA BHÁN.

A Úna ḃán, a ḃláiṫ na ndlaoiḋ ómra
Atá 'réir do ḃáis de ḃárr droċ-ċómairle,
Feuċ a ġráḋ, cia aca b'ḟearr de'n dá ċómairle
A éin i g-cliaḃán 's mé i n-áṫ na Donóige.

A Úna ḃán d'ḟágḃuiḋ tu mé i mbrón carta,
Agus cia b'áil leat ḃeiṫ tráċt air go deó fearta,
Cúilín fáinneaċ air ar ḟás suas an t-ór leaġṫa
A's go mbḟearr liom air láiṁ leat 'ná an ġlóir flaiṫis.

A Úna ḃán, ar seisean, na g-curraċán (?) cam
'S an dá ṡúil agad buḋ ċiúine d'á ndeaċaiḋ i g-ceann,
A ḃéilín an tsiúcra, mar leaṁnaċt mar ḟion 's mar ḃeóir,
Agus a ċos deas lúṫmar is tu ṡiúbalfaḋ gan ṗian i mbróig.

A Úna ḃán, mar rós i ngáirdín tu,
'S buḋ ċoinnleóir óir ar ḃórd na bainrioġan' tu,
Buḋ ċeileaḃair agus buḋ ċeólṁar ag gabail an ḃealaiġ seó ró-ṁam tu,
Agus 'sé mo ċreaċ-ṁaidne brónaċ nár pósaḋ le do ḋuḃ-ġráḋ tu.

A Úna ḃán is tu do ṁearuiġ mo ċiall
A Úna is tu ċuaiḋ go dlúṫ idir mé 'gus Dia,
A Úna, a ċraéḃ cúbarṫa, a lúibín ċasta na g-ciaḃ,
Nár ḃ'fearr dam-sa ḃeiṫ gan súiliḃ ná d'ḟeiceál ariaṁ.

whole of them or the half. I heard these stories about Tomaus Loidher from Shamus O'Hart, from Walter Scurlogue (or Sherlock), both of them dead now, and from Martin O'Brennan, or Brannan, in the County Roscommon, but I got some of the verses from a man in the island of Achill who had never heard any talk about Tomaus Loidher.

When he died he was buried, as he himself directed, in the same grave-yard and island in which Una was buried, and there grew an ash-tree out of Una's grave and another tree out of the grave of Costello, and they inclined towards one another, and they did not cease from growing until the two tops were met and bent upon one another in the middle of the graveyard, and people who saw them said they were that way still, but I was lately on the brink of Lough Cé and could not see them. I was not, however, on the island.

OONA WAUN (FAIR UNA).

O fair Una, thou blossom of the amber locks,
Thou who art after thy death from the result of ill counsel,
See, O love, which of them was the best of the two counsels,
O bird in a cage, and I in the ford of the Donogue.

O fair Una, thou has left me in grief twisted,
And why shouldst thou like to be recounting it any more for ever?
Ringleted *cooleen* upon which grew up the melted gold,
And sure I would rather be sitting beside thee than the glory of heaven.

O fair Una, said he, of the crooked skiffs (?)*
And the two eyes you have the mildest that ever went in a head,
O little mouth of the sugar, like new milk, like wine, like *b'yore,*
And O pretty active foot, it is you would walk without pain in a shoe!

O fair Una, like a rose in a garden you,
And like a candlestick of gold you were on the table of a queen,
Melodious and musical you were going this road before me,
And it is my sorrowful morning-spoil that you were not married to your dark love.

O fair Una, it is you who have set astray my senses;
O Una, it is you who went close in between me and God,
O Una, fragrant branch, twisted little curl of the ringlets,
Was it not better for me to be without eyes than ever to have seen you?

---

* Perhaps referring to the skiffs or curraghs on Loch Cé, round which so many of the MacDermotts lived.

Is fliuċ agus fuar mo ċuairt-se ċum an baile aréir,
Agus mé mo ṡuiḋe suas ar bruaċ na leapṫan liom féin,
A ġile gan gruaim ag nár luaḋaḋ an iomadaṁlaċt aċt mé
Cad as naċ bfuagruiġeann tu fuaċt na maidne ḋam féin.

Tá daoine ann san tsaoġal so ċaiṫeas di-ṁeas ar ḋúiṫċe falaṁ*
A lán de ṁaoin ṡaoġalta, agus ni buan í accu†
Ceasaċt maoine ni ḋeunfainn ná truaġ fearainn,
Aċt b'ḟearr liom ná dá ċaora da mbeiṫ'‡ Úna ágam.

Fuair mé na ceiṫre ceaṫraṁna so leanas i nDroiċ-sgríbinn, naċ raib aċt cuid de na ceaṫraṁnaib ṡuas ann. Níor ċualas féin ariaṁ na ceiṫre cinn eile seó. Is soilléir naċ é an Coisdealaċ do rinne an ceann deireannaċ aca, ar ṁód ar biṫ.

Searaiḋ agus dearcaiḋ bfuil mo ró-ġráḋ ag tíġeaċt,
Is mar ċnap-sneaċta [í] a's mar ṁil-beaċa (do) róiġeaḋ an ġrian,
Mar ċnap-sneaċta 's mar ṁil-beaċa (do) róiġeaḋ an ġrian,
Agus a ċuid 's a ċaraid is fada mé beó do ḋiaiġ.

A Úna, a ainnir, a ċaraiḋ, 's a ḋéid órḋa,
A béilín meala nár ċan riaṁ eugcóra,
B' ḟearr liom-sa beiṫ ar leabaiḋ léi 'gá síor-ṗógaḋ
'Ná mo ṡuiḋe i bflaiṫeas i g-cáṫaoir na Trionóide.

Ġluais mé tríd buaile mo ċarad aréir,
A's ní bfuair mé féin fuaraḋ ná fliuċaḋ mo béil
'S é dubairt an stuaḋ-ċailín gruama a's madar as a méar
Mo ṫri truaiġe ni (i) n-uaigneas do casaḋ liom ṫu (féin).

Ceiṫre Úna ceiṫre Áine, ceiṫre Máire 's ceiṫre Nóra
Na ceiṫre mná buḋ ceiṫre breáċta bi (i g-) ceiṫre ceardaib na
Fóḋla,
Ceiṫre tairngiḋe a's ceiṫre sáb ag ceiṫre clársaib cóṁra§
Ceiṫre gráin air na ceiṫre mnáib naċ dtiubraḋ a g-ceiṫre gráḋ
d'á g-ceiṫre pógaib.

---

*=folaṁ. †=aca. ‡ beiṫ'=" beiḋeaḋ," i g-Connaċtaib.

§ " Ceiṫre társaiġ a gceiṫre tráġ a g-ceiṫre claraiġ cóṁanra," 'san MS.

It's wet and cold was my visit to the village last night,
And I sitting up on the brink of the couch by myself,
O brightness without gloom, to whom the many were not betrothed but [only] I,
Wherefore proclaimest thou not the cold of the morning to myself.

There are people in this world who throw disrespect upon an empty estate
[Having] a quantity of worldly goods [themselves], though they have them not lastingly,
Complaint over [lack of] goods or lament for land I would not make;
I would rather than two sheep if I had Una (*i.e.* "a lamb," a play on the word).

I found the following four stanzas in a bad manuscript in which were only a few of the above verses. I never heard these other four myself. It is plain it was not the Costello who made the last one of them, at all events.

Stand ye and look ye is my very love a-coming,
She is like a ball of snow and like bee's honey which the sun would freeze
Like a ball of snow and like bee's honey the sun would freeze;
And my portion (*i.e.* my love) and my friend, it is long that I am alive after you.

O Una, O maiden, O friend, and O golden tooth,
O little mouth of honey that never uttered injustice,
I had rather be beside her on a couch, ever kissing her,
Than be sitting in heaven in the chair of the Trinity.

I passed through the byre* of my friends last night;
I never got any refreshment or [even] the wetting of my mouth.
'Twas what the frowning high-shouldered (?) girl said, and madder on her fingers,
" My three pities that it was not in a solitude I met yourself."

Four Unas, four Annies, four Marys and four Noras,
The four women, the four finest were in the four quarters of Fola (Ireland)
Four nails and four saws to four boards of coffin,
Four hates on the four women who would not give their four loves off their four kisses.

---

* Or perhaps through the town of Boyle, *i.e.* *Búille* not *buaile.*

Ṫug mé cóip de'n Ċeann Duḃ Díleas ċeana, ameasg na n-abrán ar ar ġlaoḋ mé "Abráin Ocáideaċa," agus d'innis mé fáṫ a ḋeunta, agus ṫaisbéan mé gur eugsaṁuil ar fad é ó'n g-cóipín gearr dé do bí i g-cló le O h-Argadáin. Caiṫfiḋ mé anois an treas cóip ċur síos. Tá sí gearr simpliḋe agus binn. Is cosṁúil gur sine an ċóip seó 'ná aimsir an Ċearbalánaiġ. Tá sé seo níos cosṁúile le ceaṫramnaiḃ Uí h-Argadáin ná an t-abrán do ṫug mé ann san g-ceud-ċaibidil.

CEANN DUḂ ḊÍLEAS.

Tá mná an ḃaile seo ar buile 's ar buaiḋreaḋ
Ag tarraing a ngruaige 's 'gá leigean le gaoiṫ,
Ní ġlacfaiḋ siad sgafaire d'ḟearaiḃ na tuaiṫe,
Go dtéiḋ siad 'san ruaig le buaċaillíḃ an ríġ.

Ceann duḃ díleas díleas díleas
Ceann duḃ díleas druid liom anall,
Ceann duḃ is gile 'ná 'n eala 's an ḟaoilean
Is duine gan ċroiḋe naċ dtiuḃraḋ ḋuit gráḋ.

A ógánaiġ uasail uasail uasail
Geoḃaiḋ tu duais a's fuirig go lá,
Geoḃaiḋ tu sgioból a's urlár an ḃuailte
Agus cead do ḃeiṫ suas go n-éireóċaiḋ an lá.

Ceann duḃ díleas díleas díleas,
Ceann duḃ díleas, druid liom análl,
Ceann Duḃ is gile 'ná 'n eala 's an ḟaoilean
Is duine gan ċroiḋe naċ dtiuḃraḋ ḋuit gráḋ.

Ḃéarfaiḋ mé ann so abrán air a nglaoḋtar an Páistín Fionn. Tá abrán de'n ainm sin i leaḃar an h-Argadánaiġ aċt ní'l aon líne ann cosṁúil leis an dán so. Ní'l sé ró ṡoilléir cad air a bfuil an dán so ag trácht. Ḃí sgeul i dtaoiḃ mná éigin a ṫáinig cleaṫaire .i. rógaire le na fuadaċ leis, aċt ċuir sí a culaiḋ féin ar ḋuine éigin eile, agus níor ḟuaduiġ an "cleaṫaire cam" an duine ceart leis. Ní ṫig linn an sean-sgeul ḟáġail anois, tá faitcíos orm go bfuil sé caillte. Is cinnte mé gur i dtaoiḃ ruid ḟírinniġ a ṫárla aon uair aṁáin ameasg na ndaoine, do cumaḋ níos mó 'ná leaṫ de na sean abránaiḃ seó, aċt ní ṫig linn fáġail amaċ anois cad iad na h-ocáidiḋe faoi a n-dearnaḋ iad. Is cos-ṁúil go bfuil dá abrán measgṫa suas ann san abrán so, an dá ċeud ḃeursa ag trácht ar an iarraiḋ do rinne an Cleaṫaire cam leis an bPáistín Fionn .i. cailín bán, d'ḟuadaċ leis, agus ar an g-

I gave a version of the Cann Dhu Dheelisn, or Darling Black Head, amongst the songs which I called "Occasional," and told the reason of its composition, and showed that it was quite different from the short little copy of it that was printed by Hardiman. I must now give the third version of it; it is short, simple and sweet. It is probable that this copy is older than Carolan's time. This song is more like Hardiman's stanzas than the one given in the first chapter.

DARLING BLACK HEAD.

(ANOTHER VERSION).

The women of this village are in madness and trouble,
Pulling their hair and letting it go with the wind,
They will not accept a gallant of the men of the country
Until they go into the rout with the boys of the king.*

Black Head, Darling, Darling, Darling,
Black Head, Darling, move over to me,
Black Head, brighter than swan and than seagull,
He's a man without heart gives not love to thee.

O youth well-born, well born, well-born
Thou shalt get a reward, and remain till day,
Thou shalt get barn and threshing floor,
And leave to be up till the day shall rise.

Black Head, Darling, Darling, Darling,
Black Head, Darling, move over to me,
Black Head, brighter than swan or than seagull,
He's a man without heart gives not love to thee.

I shall here give a song called the Paustyeen Finn.† There is a song of that name in Hardiman's book, but there is not one line in it resembling this poem. It is not very clear what this poem is about. There was a story about some woman that a "clahirya," or rogue (?) came to carry off with him, but she put her own garments on someone else, and the crooked "clahirya" did not carry off the right person with him. We cannot find the old story now; I am afraid it is lost. I am sure it was about some true event or other that once hap-

* This seems to mean that the girls said they would not marry anyone who had not fought with and routed the king's troops. All these old songs, however, are very obscure.

† This word, as in the name of the celebrated warrior, Finn MacCool, is pronounced like "Finn" in Connacht and the North, but something like "Fewn" (rhyming with tune) in parts of Munster and Scotland. Hence the diversity of spelling we meet with in the Anglicized Ossianic tales.

caoi ann ar ṁeall sí é, agus tá an ċuid leanas ag molaḋ sgéiṁe an ṗáistín, agus ann sin deir duine éigin—an "Cleaṫaire cam" b'éidir—nár ċóir a ċroċaḋ ar son an ṗáistín, mar d'imṫiġ sí leis go toilteannaċ. Da g-cruinneóċaiḋe na sean-aḃráin seó ceud bliaḋain no ceud bliaḋain go leiṫ, ó ṡoin, i n-éinḟeaċt leis na sgeultaiḃ ḃaineas leó, ni ḃeiḋeaḋ na bearnaḋa móra ionnta, agus ni ḃeiḋeaḋ siad ċoṁ briste suas agus ċoṁ do-ṫuigṫe a's atá siad anois. Is truaġ ḟíor-ṁór é nár cruinniġeaḋ aḃránaċt agus bárdaċt agus sgeuluiġeaċt na ndaoine—ní'l mé ag tráċt ann so ar aḃránaċt agus filiḋe aċt na mbárd--a ḃfad ó, agus do ḋeunfaḋ siad an ciste agus an stór is luaċṁaire agus is spéiseaṁlad'á ḃfuil le ḟáġail ameasg na náisiún labras teanga "Ċeilteaċ." Tá sé ró ṁall ann san lá anois, le dul d'á g-cruinniuġaḋ agus d'á mbailiuġaḋ óir bainiḋ leaṫ no trí ceaṫraṁna de na h-aḃránaiḃ is fearr le ceart lár na h-Éireann agus leis na condaéiḃ sin ann naċ laḃairṫear aċt fíorḃeagán Gaeḋeilge andiú. Má ṫéiḋmid a ḃfad siar cois na mara ameasg na sléiḃteaḋ agus na n-iasgaire, geoḃamaoid daoine go deiṁin labras Gaeḋeilge de ġnáṫ, aċt ní'l aca anois mórán eile taoḃ amuiġ de na h-aḃránaiḃ agus de na sgeultaiḃ do ḃí coitċionn ann a measg féin, agus d'éiriġ cois na fairrge, aċt tá sgeuluiġeaċt agus bárdaċt na coda is saiḋḃre agus is deaġ-ṁúinte agus na n-daoine is mó eólas agus léiġean, imṫiġṫe agus caillte anois, mar atá i gcondaé na Miḋe agus na h-iar-Ṁiḋe agus i gceart-lár na h-Éireann ar fad, i gcondaé Longfoṙd, Roscomáin, Luimniġ, Tiobraid Árann agus plúr na h-Éireann. Faraor geur! Is caill ḋóċreidte é.

An Páistín Fionn.

Ceann deireannaċ de'n tSáṫairn músglóċad an greann,
Ṫáinig mo deirḃṡiúr ċugam go caoiṁeaṁuil fann,
"Tiucfaiḋ sé ċugainn an Cleaṫaire cam
Agus béarfaiḋ sé mise 'sa' ḃ-fuadac."

Bain ṫusa ḋíot eudaiġ do ċuirp a's do ċinn,
Agus cuir ort mo hata 's mo ċulaiḋ úr ḋonn,
Má ṫigeann sé ċugainn an cleaṫaire cam
Is mise ḃéiḋeas leis ann sa' ḃfuadaċ.

pened amongst the people that more than half of these old songs were composed, but we cannot now find out what were the occasions on which they were made. It is probable that there are two songs mixed up in this one, the two first verses speaking of the attempt which the crooked clahirya made to carry off with him the Paustyeen Finn, or fair-haired childeen, and of the way in which she deceived him, and what follows is praising the beauty of the Paustyeen, and then somebody is saying—perhaps the crooked clahirya—that he ought not to be hanged for the Paustyeen because she went with him willingly. If these old songs had been collected a hundred or a hundred and fifty years ago, together with the stories that belong to them, these great gaps would not occur in them, and they would not be so broken up and so unintelligible as they are now. It is a really great pity that the song and poetry and story of the people—I am not now talking of the song and poetry of the bards—were not collected long ago, and they would make the most valuable and interesting store and treasure amongst the nations that speak a Celtic language. It is now too late in the day to go gathering or collecting them, for half or three-fourths of the best songs belong to the middle of Ifeland, or to those counties in which only a very little Irish is spoken to-day. If we go far back beside the sea, amongst the mountains and the fishermen, we will find people who habitually, indeed, speak Irish, but they have not much now outside of the songs and stories that were common in their own midst and rose beside the sea; but the stories and bardism of the wealthiest and best educated portion of the country, the portion of most knowledge and learning, are now gone and lost, such as those of the counties of Meath and Westmeath, and all the central parts of Ireland, Longford, Roscommon, Tipperary and the flower of Erin. Alas! it is an incredible loss.

THE PAUSTYEEN FINN, OR THE FAIR-HAIRED CHILDEEN.

At the last end of the Saturday I shall waken the fun,
My sister came to me mildly and weak,
"He will come to us, the crooked clahirya,
  And will bring me off by violence."

"Do you take off the dress of your body and your head
And put on my hat and my new brown suit,
If he come to us, the crooked clahirya,
  It's I shall be carried off by him."

Níl de ṁaoin an tsaoġail agam aċt aon deirḃsiúr aṁáin
agus ní "péic" an doṁain buḋ ṁaiṫ liom í ḟáġail,
ní ḃéarfainn-se sgilling ar m'ḟortún go bráṫ
Muna* dtig liom a ráḋ gur liom féin í.

Nuair ċuaiḋ mé amaċ leis an bPáirtín Fionn
Tá me lán-ċinnte gur ḋúbluiġ mé an greann,
Ċuir mé mo láṁ ṫairsti a's ḋeasuiġ sí liom,
A's d'ḟreastail mé an t-am ḃí 'sa' láṫair.

Gráḋ le m'anam í, an Páirtín Fionn,
A croiḋe 's a h-anam ḃeiṫ fáisgṫe liom,
Dá ċíċ ġeala mar ḃláṫ na dtom
'S a píob mar an eala lá Márta.

Nuair d'éiriġ sí ar maidin an Páirtín Fionn
"A ċuisle na g-carad créad ḋeunfas tu liom?"
"A ṡiúir" ar sa mise, "taḃair d'aṫair ar faill,
'S má ṫogruiġeannt† tu aiṫris do sgeul ḋó.

Cad do b'áil daoiḃ mo ċroċaḋ fá 'n b-Páirtín Fionn,
A's gur ar mo neaṁ-ṫoil tugaḋ mé ann,
Ní éigin d'á n-aiṁ-ḋeoin do rinne mé ann,
Aċt le lán-ṫoil a h-aṫar 's a máṫar.

Dá mbéiḋinn-se i dteaċ folaṁ gan aoin-neaċ ann,
Gaoṫ ṁór agus fearṫainn dá séideaḋ os ár g-cionn,
Gan neaċ do ḃeiṫ 'm' aice, aċt an Páirtín Fionn
Is cinnte go n-ólfainn a sláinte.

Gan ḃád ná coite do ḋeunfainn snáṁ,
Gan gunna gan ṗiostal do ḋeunfainn láṁ,‡
Níl aoin-ḟear a ḃainfeaḋ le mo ḋeirḃsiúir aṁáin
Naċ ndeunfainn púdar d'á ċnáṁaiḃ.

Is é an port agus ní h-iad na focail do rinne clú an aḃráin seó, mar ċiḋmíd le mórán eile aca.

Seó anois comráḋ idir buaċaill agus cailín, ann a ḃfuil an cailín ag cur aṁrais ann a ḋearḃuġaḋ go dtug sé gráḋ síorruiḋe ḋí. Is an-ċoitċionn aḃráin de'n ċineál so, agus cuirim an ceann so síos mar ṡompla ar mórán eile.

* "Mar," 'san MS.

† "eagraiġeann tu," 'san MS. focal naċ dtuigim.

‡="Láṁaċ" .i. sgaoileaḋ gunna?

I have not of the goods of this life but one sister only,
And it is not a rake of the world I would wish to have her.
I would not give a shilling for my fortune for ever
    Unless I can say that she is my own.

When I went out with the Paustyeen Finn
I am certain sure that I doubled the fun ;
I put my arm round her and to me she clung
    And I served the time that was present (?).

The love of my soul is the Paustyeen Finn,
Her heart and her soul to be squeezed to me,
Two breasts, bright like the blossom of the bushes,
    And her neck like the swan on a March day.

When she rose in the morning, the Paustyeen Finn,
"O pulse of the friends, what wilt thou do with me?"
"O sister," said I, "take your father on an occasion
    And if you choose tell him your story."

Why do you wish to hang me for the Paustyeen Finn?
And sure against my will I was brought into it.
It was not violence against their wish I did there
    But with the full consent of her father and mother.

If I were to be in an empty house without anyone in it,
Great wind and rain blowing over our heads,
Without anyone to be near me but the Paustyeen Finn
    It is certain that I would drink her health.

Without a boat or a cot I would make a rowing,
Without a gun or a pistol I would make a shooting.
There is no man would touch my one little sister*
    That I would not make powder of his bones.

It is the air and not the words which has made the fame of this song, as we see is the case with many more.

Here, now, is a conversation between a boy and a girl in which she doubts the reality of his protestations of eternal love. Songs of this kind are very common, and I put this one down as an example of many more—

---

* Sister is often used, not as a term of relationship, but, as here, of affection.

Uċ a Úna.

(Eisean).

Uċ a Úna an tinn no an dúḃaċ leat
Mise ag deunaṁ cúṁa am' aonar,
'S dá mbraiṫfinn do ḋúṫraċt ann mo ċodlaḋ ná mo ṫúireaċt
Do ḋeunfainn rún go h-eug ort.

Is iongantaċ liom-sa ṫu ḃeiṫ bonn-os-cionn liom
'S mé ḃeiṫ lán de'n dúil ḃeiṫ réiḋ leat,
'S dá dtiucfaḋ* ċúgainn a ṁúirnín muiriġin ná cúram
Is aṫair mé ṁúinfeaḋ léiġean dó.

(Ise).

A óganaiġ ṁúinte na labarṫa ciúna
Taiṫniġeann do ċlú a's do ṁéin liom,
Níor ḃ'aite leat súgraḋ dart† m'ḟallaing 'ná liom-sa
Aċt ar eagla ṫu ḃeiṫ breugaċ.

Mar is sgafaire ṫu tá meanmnaċ súgaċ
'Spalpaḋ na mionn 's na n-éiṫeaċ,
'S go mb' eagalaċ liom dá leanfainn-se ṫu
Gur casaḋ fá ċúṁa do ḋeunfainn.

(Eisean ag freagairt).

A ġráḋ 'gus a ċuid go bráṫ ná tuig
Go ndeunfainn ḋo ṁalairt de ċéile,
Go n-iompuiġ' an ṁuir ar fad 'nna fuil,
'S go ngaḃann na cnuic fá ċéile.

Go ḃfásfaiḋ biolar tríd lár na teineaḋ,
'S go dtig na bric d'á éiliuġaḋ,
'S go g-caillid na druid' ar fad a n-guib,
'S go ndeunfaiḋe lon de'n ċéirsiġ.

Is abrán Connaċtaċ an Ċúilín no an "Ċúilḟionn" agus beir O hArgadáin dúinn é. Tá cóip Ṁuiṁneaċ i gcló mar an g céadna. Aċt ḃéarfaiḋ mé ann so cóip eile do fuair mé i láiṁ-sgríḃinn atá agam do ḃí sgríoḃṫa i g-condaé an Chláir, atá eugsaṁuil ar fad ó'n dá ċóip eile. Fágaim amaċ dá rann dé atá ar aon ḟocal, beag-naċ, leis na ḃéarsaiḃ i leaḃar Uí Ḋálaiġ, i ḃfiliḋeaċt na Cúige

---

* "dá dtigid" 'san MS. droċ-ḟoirm naċ ḃfeicimid go minic annsna sean-abránaiḃ seó. D'aṫraiġ mé an líne seo beagán.

† "air," san MS.

UGH, O UNA.

[HE].

Ugh, O Una, do you think it a sickly or sorrowful thing
  Me to be making melancholy alone?
And if I were to observe your earnestness in my sleeping or my waking
  I would make a secret-love of you (or set my heart on you?) till death.

I think it wonderful, you to be upside down (*i.e.* fallen out) with me,
  And I full of desire to be reconciled to you;
And if there were to come to us, my dear, a family or a care,
  A father I who would teach them learning.

[SHE].

O learned youth of the quiet speeches
  Your fame and your mien please me,
By my cloak! sport were no more agreeable to you than to me,
  But for fear of you being false.

For you are a gallant, who is high-spirited, merry,
  Taking-rashly oaths and perjury;
And, sure, I would be afraid if I were to follow you,
  That it is a return under melancholy I would make.

[HE].

My love, and my portion, do not think for ever
  That I would ever exchange you for another consort;
Until the sea change entirely into blood,
  And until the hills go under each other.

Until watercress shall grow through the middle of the fire,
  And until the trout come to sue for it;
Until the starlings shall altogether lose their bills,
  And, until a blackbird is made of the thrush.

The Cooleen, or Coolun, literally the "Cúl Fhionn," or fair-haired cool, *i.e.* back-hair, is a Connacht song, and Hardiman gives it to us, and there is a Munster version in print also; but I shall here give another copy which I have, which I found in a manuscript of mine, written in the County Clare, which is altogether different from the other two copies. I omit two ranns of it which are almost on one word with

Muṁan, 'san abrán "A Ṁáire 'gus a ċuisle," ag leaṫanaċ 224; agus tá dá rann eile scríocṫe i ríoċt naċ dtig liom a léiġeaḋ, aċt ag so an ċuid eile ḋé. Ní'l aon abrán i n-Éirinn is mo clú 'ná an Ċúilḟionn agus ar an ádbar sin is rud fíor-usáideaċ é na cóipeanna eugsaṁla ḋé do ḃailiuġaḋ agus do ċur i g-cló. Deir O Daláiġ gur ċuairtiġ sé an Ṁúṁan ar fad agus naċ bfuair se aċt na trí rainn do ṫug sé. Ḃí mise níos áḋaṁla.

An Ċúilḟionn.

Ceó meala lá seaca, ar ċoilltiḃ duḃa daraiġe
A's gráḋ gan ċeilt atá agam duit a ḃáin-ċnis na ngeal-ċíoċ,
Do ċom seang, do ḃeul tana, a's do ċúilín ḃí cas mín,
A's a ċéad-ḟearc ná tréig mé, as gur ṁéaduiġ tu ar m'aicíd.

A's cia ċiḋfeaḋ mo ġráḋ-sa ar ċeart-lár an aonaiġ,
'S gur marḃaḋ na mílte ógánaċ le pósaiḃ a h-eudain.
A gruaiḋ mar an g-cocan, 's í buḋ ḃreáġṫa ar doṁan sgéiṁe
A's gur dóiġ le gaċ sprionán gur ab áilleán dó féin í.

An té ċiḋfeaḋ an Ċúilḟionn 's í ag siúḃal ar na bántaiḃ
Ar maidin laé saṁraiḋ 's an drúċt ar a brógaiḃ.
'S a liaċt ógánaċ súil-ġlas ḃíos ag tnúṫ le na pósaḋ
Aċt ní ḃfáġaiḋ siad mo rún-sa ar an g-cúntas is dóiġ leó.

A Neiliḋ, mo ġráḋ-sa, an dtiocfá liom faoi ḟléiḃtiḃ.
Ag ól fíona a's bolcáin* a's bainnne an ġaḃair ġlé-gil.
Ceól fada a's imirt do ṫaḃarfainn le d' raé ḋuit,
A's cead dul a' codlaḋ i mbrollaċ mo léine.

Ag so anois an ceaṫramaḋ cóip de'n abrán clúṫamail ceudna, atá eugsaṁail ar fad ó na trí cinn eile. Fágaim amaċ an dara agus an tríoṁaḋ rann óir tá siad ann san gcóip do ṫug O hArgadáin, is é sin na rainn ṫosuiġeas "Gibé ċiḋfeaċ an Ċúilḟionn," agus "An cuimin leat an lá úd."

* Cineál uisge-beaṫa, creidim. Taisbéanaiḋ an focal so go ḃfuil an cóip seó de'n Ċúilḟionn sean go leór, óir is fada o ḃí aon tráċt ar "bolcán." Ċiḋmíd an focal so fá ḋó 'san abrán cliúṫaċ sin "Magaiḋ Láidir."

the verses in O'Daly's book, "The Poetry of Munster," in the song "A Waurya gus a hushla" at p. 224, and there are two other verses torn in a way that I cannot read them, but here is the other part of it. There is no song in Erin more famous than the Cooleen, and for that reason, it is an exceedingly useful thing to collect and print the various copies of it. O'Daly says that after hunting through Munster he only found the three verses of this song which he has given. I was more fortunate.

THE COOLEEN, OR COOLUN.

A honey mist on a day of frost, in a dark oak wood,
And love for thee in my heart in me, thou bright, white, and good;
Thy slender form, soft and warm, thy red lips apart,
Thou hast found me, and hast bound me, and put grief in my heart.

In fair-green and market, men mark thee, bright, young, and merry.
Though thou hurt them like foes with the rose of thy blush of the berry;
Her cheeks are a poppy,* her eye it is Cupid's helper,
But each foolish man dreams that its beams for himself are.

Whoe'er saw the Cooleen in a cool dewy meadow
On a morning in summer in sunshine and shadow;
All the young men go wild for her, my childeen, my treasure,
But now let them go mope, they've no hope to possess her.

Let us roam, O my darling, afar through the mountains,
Drink milk of the goat, wine and bulcaun in fountains;
With music and play every day from my lyre,
And leave to come rest on my breast when you tire.†

Here is now the fourth copy of the same renowned song, which is altogether different from the other three. I leave out the second and third stanzas of it, for they are in the version which Hardiman gave; those are the stanzas beginning, "Whosoever would see the Coolin," and "Do you remember the day."

---

* This is the only song in which I remember meeting the word *cocán*, which, I think, means "poppy," applied to a girl's cheeks.

† This translation is nearly in the metre of the original.

Literally. Mist of honey on day of frost over dark woods of oak, And love without concealment I have for thee, O fair skin of the white breasts. Thy form slender, thy mouth thin, and thy cooleen twisted, smooth. And O first love, forsake me not, and sure thou hast increased my disease.

And who would see my love upon the middle of the fair, And sure the thou-

An Ċúilḟionn. (Cóip eile).

A's éiriġ do ṡuiḋe a ḃuaċaill a's gleus dam mo ġearrán
Go raċaiḋ mé go luaṫ* ag cur tuairisg mo ḋian-ġráḋ,
A's tá sí d'á luaḋ liom ó ḃí sí 'nna leanaḃán
'S gur ḃuḋ ḃinne liom naoi n-uaire í 'ná cuaċ a's 'ná orgáin.†

An cuiṁin leat an oiḋċe úd do ḃíomar ag an ḃfuinneóig
Ann a rug tu ar láiṁ orm 's gur ḟáisg tu orm boróg (?)
Do ṡín mé le do ṫaoiḃ, 's ann mo ċroiḋe ní raiḃ urċóid,
A's do ḃí mé ann do ċóṁluadar no g-cuala mé an ḟuiseóg.

'Sí mo ṡúr í, 'sí mo rún í, 'sí mo ġráḋ í, 'sí mo ḋalta,
'S í grianán na ḃfear óg í gaċ aon lá 'san tseaċtṁain.
Tá a gruaiḋ mar an rós a's a píob mar an eala.
Sé mo ċúṁa gan mé i gcóṁnuiḋe mar a g-córaiġeann sí a leaḃaiḋ.

Ní'l airgead ní'l ór agam, ní'l cóta, ní'l léine,
Ní'l piġin ann mo ṗóca 's go ḃfóiriḋ Mac Dé orm,
Do ġeall mé faoi ḋó ḋuit, sul a ṗóg mé do ḃéilín
A ṁaiġre an ċúil ómraiġ naċ bpósfainn le m' raé ṫu.

A ṁuirnín a's a annsact bí díleas a's bí daingeann,
A's ná tréig-se rún do ċroiḋe-stiġ mar ġeall ar [a] ḃeiṫ dealḃ‡
Do ḃéarfainn an bioblа§ a's niḋ ar biṫ ar talaṁ
Go dtiúḃraiḋ Mac Dé cuid na h-oiḋċe ḋúinn le cataḋ.

A Ṁúirnín a's a annsaċt do|| ṁeall tu mé i dtús m'óige
Le do ċluainiġeaċt ṁín ṁánla gur ġeall tu mé ṗósaḋ,
Má ṫug mo ċroiḋe gean duit dar liom-sa gur leór sin,
A's gur ḟág tu i leanndúḃ mé ar teaċt an tratnóna.

---

sands of youths were slain with the roses of her face, Her cheeks like the poppy, and she was the finest in beauty of the world, And sure every fopling thinks that she is his own darling.

He who would see the Cooleen and she walking on the meadows Of a morning on a day in summer, and the dew on her shoes. And all the grey-eyed youths who are envious to marry her. But they shall not get my darling as easily as they think. (*Literally*, on the account that is hope with them).

O Nelly, my love, wouldst thou come with me beneath the mountain, Drinking wine and bulcaun (a kind of spirits?) and the milk of the white goat. Long-drawn music and play I would give thee during thy life; And leave to go sleep in the bosom of my shirt.

---

* "Go luaċ mo" 'san MS, rud naċ dtuigim.
† "na narragain" 'san MS. focal naċ dtuigim.
‡ dealḃ=falaṁ no boċt. § "an biobla seoċ" 'san MS. Ní ṫuigim an "seoċ" so. || "le nar meall tu" 'san MS.

THE COOLUN.

(ANOTHER VERSION).

And rise up lad, and get ready for me my nag,
Until I go quickly to enquire for my desperately-loved,
And she is betrothed to me since the time she was a little child,
And, sure, I thought her nine times more melodious than cuckoo or organ.

Do you remember that night that we were at the window
When you caught my hand and squeezed a pressure (?) on it ?
I stretched myself at thy side, and in my heart there was no harm,
And I was in thy company until I heard the lark.

She is my sister, she is my secret,* she is my love, she is my betrothed (?)
She is the greeanawn (sunny-chamber) of the young men every day in the week;
Her countenance is like the rose, and her neck like the swan,
'Tis my sorrow I am not always where she dresses her couch.

I have no silver, I have no gold, have no coat, have no shirt;
Have no penny in my pocket—and may the Son of God relieve me,
I promised thee twice before I kissed thy little mouth,
O maiden of the amber cool, that I would not marry thee during my life.

My sweetheart, my affection, be faithful, and be firm,
And do not forsake the secret love of your inner heart on account of him to be poor;
I would take the Bible (as oath) or any (other) thing on earth,
That the Son of God will give us our nights' portion to eat.

My sweetheart, my affection, you deceived me in the beginning of my youth,
With your soft pleasant roguishness, sure, you promised to marry me,
If my heart gave you love, I think myself that that is enough,
And, sure, you left me in melancholy on the coming of evening.

---

* Rún which literally means "secret" is, in these songs, often used in the sense of sweetheart, as in "Eileen Aroon," *i.e.* "Eileen O secret (love)."

Fágaim ar m'fallaing gur fada liom uaim ad Dóṁnaċ
Go ḃfeicfiḋ mé an ainnir ag éiriġe amaċ ar na bóiṫriḃ,
Triallfaiḋ mé ċum aifrinn mar a mbéiḋ mo stór-sa,
——— Sgeul cinnte gur ḟág sí m'inntinn buaiḋearṫa.

Bhéarfaiḋ me ann so cuid d'abrán an ċlúṫamail eile, d'á dtug O hArgadáin trí rainn faoi ainm "Casaḋ an t Sugáin." Fuair mise é faoi ainm an "Súisín Bán."

An Súisín Bán.

Má ḃíonn tu liom bí liom a ġráḋ ġeal mo ċroiḋe
Má ḃíonn tu liom bí liom do ló gus d'oiḋċ,'
Má bíonn tu liom bí liom gaċ orlaċ ann do ċroiḋe
'S é mo leun a's mo lom naċ liom traṫnóna ṫu mar ṁnaoi.

An g-cluin tu* mé a Ġiolla tá ag iarraiḋ gráḋ,
Fill a-ḃaile arís a's fan bliaḋain eile mar táir,
Ṫáinig me asteaċ i dteaċ a raiḃ gráḋ geal mo ċroiḋe
A's ċuir an ċailleaċ amaċ ar ċasaḋ an tsugáin mé.

B'ait liom bean a d'fanfaḋ a bliaḋain le n-a gráḋ
B'ait liom bean a d'fanfaḋ bliaḋain uile agus a lá,
Níor ḃ'ait liom an ḃean ḃeiḋeaḋ leat-sa agus liomsa arís ar ball.
'S í mo ġráḋ an ḃean a d'fanfaḋ ar an aon stáid aṁáin.

A's cad é an cat marḃ do ṡeól ann san tír seó mé
A's a liaċt cailín deas d'ḟágḃaiḋ mé mo ḋéiġ,
Ni truimide mise sin, s ni buaileaḋ† orm é,
A's gur minic do ḃain bean slat do ḃuailfeaḋ í féin.

A's ṡíos i Sligeaċ ċuir me eólas ar na mnáiḃ,
Agus ṡiar i nGaillim d'ól mé leó fá mo ṡáiṫ, etc.

Is é faṫ an abráin seó, bárd do ṫug gráḋ do ṁnaoi óig agus ṫáinig sé asteaċ 'san tiġ ann a raiḃ sí féin agus a máṫair le tuitim na h-oiḋċe. B'olc leis an trean ṁnaoi a ṫiġeaċt, agus smuaín si aici féin cia an ċaoi do b'ḟearr le n-a ċur amaċ arís. Agus ṫosaiġ sí ag casaḋ sugain no rópa tuiġe. Ċoinniġ sise an tuiġe agus ċuir sí an bárd g'á ċasaḋ. Bí an bárd dul ar a ċúl réir mar ḃí an sugán ag faduġaḋ no go ndeaċaiḋ sé amaċ ar an

* "gluin tu leat mé" 'san MS.
† "ni buala" MS. rud nac ḃfuil soiléir.

I leave it on (*i.e.*, swear by) my mantle that I think it long from me the Sunday is,
Till I shall see the maiden rising out on the roads;
I shall journey to Mass where my treasure shall be—
A sure tale it is, that she has left my mind troubled.

I shall give here part of another renowned song, of which Hardiman gave three verses under the name of "The Twisting of the Rope." I found it under the name of the Soosheen Bawn, or White Coverlet.

THE SOOSHEEN BAWN.

If thou art mine, be mine, white love of my heart:
If thou art mine, be mine by day and by night;
If thou art mine, be mine every inch in thy heart,
And my misfortune and misery that thou art not with me in the evening for wife.

[The maiden answers:]

"Do you hear me, you gilly, who are seeking love?
Return home again, and remain another year as you are."

[The harper says:]

I came into a house where the bright love of my heart was,
And the hag put me out a-twisting of the suggaun.

I would like a woman who would wait her year for her love;
I would like a woman who would wait a whole year and her day;
I would not like the woman who would be with you and again, on the spot, with me:
My love is the woman who would remain in the one state only.

And what was the dead cat which guided me into this country,
And the numbers of pretty girls I left behind me?
I am not the heavier for that, and I was not beaten by it,
And sure a woman often cut a rod would beat herself.

And down in Sligo I gained a knowledge of women,
And back in Galway I drank with them my enough, etc.

'Tis the cause of this song—a bard who gave love to a young woman, and he came into the house where she herself was with her mother at the fall of night. The old woman was angry, him to come, and she thought to herself what would be the best way to put him out again, and she began twisting a suggaun, or straw rope. She

doras faoi ḋeire, agus é ag síor-ċasaḋ. Nuair fuair an tsean bean amuiġ é, d'éiriġ sí de ṗreab agus ḃuail sí an doras ann a eúdan. Ṫeilg sí amaċ an ċláirseaċ ann sin ċuige ṫríd an ḃfuinneóig agus duḃairt leis ḃeiṫ 'g imṫeaċt. Is é "Naċ é an caṫ marḃ ċas ann na h-áite-si me" ceud líne de'n aḃrán i leaḃar Ui Hargadáin, líne nár ṫuig mé ariaṁ, aċt is dóiġ gur loċt an focal "caṫ," agus gur "cat" mar fuair mise é buḋ ċeart do ḃeiṫ ann, agus gur b'ionnann "cat marḃ" agus droċ-áḋ, i g-canaṁain an ḃáird.

Ag so anois aḃrán ainmneaṁail eile ċualas féin ó ḟean-duine. Fuair mé cóip dé i sgríḃinn éigin a duḃairt gur b'é Dóṁnall Faire (no Fairre?) O Gormáin, cia bé ar biṫ an bárd sin, do rinne é.

BRIĠID A STÓIR.

A Ḃríġid a stóir ná pós an sean duine
Aċt pós fear óg 's é d'oileaḋ leanḃ duit,
Do ṡínfeaḋ síos go caoin ar leabaiḋ leat
Do ḃéarfaḋ póg no dó ar maidin duit.

Is truaġ a Ḃríġid naċ bás do fuaras
Sul a ṫug mé gráḋ ċoṁ buan duit,
D'ḟág tu m' inntinn claoiḋte buaiḋriġṫe
Mar an crann críoṫain 's an ġaoṫ g'á luasgaḋ.

Dá mbeiḋeaḋ an tír seo mar buḋ ċóir dí
I g-caisleán aoibinn do ḃeiṫeá do ċóṁnuiḋe,
Ḃeiḋ' Gaill a's Gaoḋail ag déanaṁ bróin tríot,
'S ni ḃéiḋ mé féin* ag plé níos mó leat.

Do ġeall tu daṁ-sa, 's do rinn' tu breug liom,
Go mbeiṫeá liom-sa ag Cró na g-caoraċ,
Do leig mé fead agus míle glaoḋ ort
'S ni ḃfuaireas ann aċt uain ag méiḋliġ†

'S do ġaḃ tu ṫarm go dorċa déiġeannaċ
'S do ġaḃ tu ṫarm, a's solas an laé ann,
Dá dtiucfá [féin] asteaċ do m'ḟeuċaint
Deaṁan fiarán (?) do ḃeiḋeaḋ‡ agam féin leat.

---

* "'S go mbiaḋ liom fein a beiṫ plé" 'san MS., naċ dtuigim.

† "mbéiliḋ"—'san MS.

‡ "Diún fiarán do ḃaċ agam" etc. 'san MS., no mar ċualaiḋ mise é "niún (.i. deaṁan) bean i n-Eirinn b' fearr liom féin 'ná ṫu."

held the straw, and she put the bard a-twisting it. The bard was going backwards according as the suggaun was a-lengthening, until at last he went out on the door and he ever-twisting. When the old woman found him outside she rose up of a leap and struck the door to in his face. She then flung his harp out to him through the window, and told him to be going. [The first line of this song in Hardiman's book runs, "Is it not the dead battle that twisted me into this place," a line which I never understood, but it is certain that the word *cath*, "battle," is a mistake, and that it is *cat*, "cat," as I found it, that should be in it; and, that dead cat in the language of the bard, is synonymous with bad luck].

Here now is another celebrated song which I heard myself from an old man. I also found a copy of it in a manuscript which said that it was Donal Faire, or Farire (of the watch ?) O'Gorman, whoever that bard may have been, who composed it.

BREED ASTORE.

O Breed, astore, do not marry the old man,
But marry a young man 'tis he who would rear thee a child.
Who would stretch softly on a couch beside thee;
Who would in the morning give thee a kiss or two.

'Tis a pity, O Breed, it was not death I found
Before I gave thee love so lasting.
Thou hast left my mind destroyed and troubled,
Like the aspen tree and the wind rocking it.

If this country were as it ought to be,
In a delightful castle thou wouldst be living;
Gall and Gael would be grieving, through thee,
And I, myself, shall not be pleading any longer with thee.

You promised me—and told me a falsehood—
That you would be with me at the pen of the sheep.
I let a whistle and a thousand shouts for you,
And I found nothing in it but the lambs a-bleating.

And you passed me by dark and late,
And you passed me by, and the light of the day in it.
If you would come in yourself to see me,
The demon a misunderstanding (?) I would have with you.

Ag so abrán milis fuair mé ameasg mórain d'abránaiḃ Connaċ-taċa, aċt ni ró ċosṁúil le h-abrán Connaċtaċ é, tá sé ró ḃinn. D'aṫraiġ mé an dá ċeud líne, óir ḃí siad mar so "Sí an Ḃriġdeaċ cam ḃuait Dar muica si suairc" focla nár ṫuigeas. Ḃí an t-abrán so sgríobṫa amaċ go h-an olc, agus ni ḃfuaireas aċt an ċóip seo aṁáin dé.

An Ḃriġdeach.

'S í an Ḃríġdeaċ tá uaim
An ċaoin-ḃean ṡáṁ ṡuairc
Reuil eólais na tíre í*
'S ar mo ċroiḋe ċuir sí cuan.
Dá ċíċ cruinne cruaiḋ
[Geal-ṗíob mar an cúbar]
Folt breáġ fada buiḋe
'S ar mo ċroiḋe ċuir sí cuan.

Ní hí Ḃénus tá mé ráḋ
Ná aon ḃean de na mnáiḃ
Aċt an spéirḃean ḋonn ġléġeal
Tá d'éis mo ċroiḋe (do) ċráḋ.
Ní ḟeunfad go bráċ
A h-ainm súd do ráḋ,
Siúr gairim í, 's ní ċeilim í,
Tar a maireann de ṁnáiḃ.

Teannam go dtí an sliaḃ
Ag éisteaċt leis an ḃfiaċ
Ann sna gleanntaiḃ duḃa duaiḃseaċa
Mar a labrann an fiaḋ†
Dar an leabar so ann mo láiṁ
A Ċúil áluinn na mbaċall bán
D'fanfainn leat i n-uaigneas‡
Go músglaiġeaḋ an lá.

---

* Dúbailtear an líne seo .i. treas líne gaċ rainn, nuair seinn-tear é, aċt níor sgríob mise dúbalta é. Ḃí an t-abrán so ró ċruaillighte agus d'aṫruiġ mise cuid ṁaiṫ ann, naċ dtaisbéanaim 's na nótaiḃ, óir buḋ ró iomadaṁail na loċta sgrioḃnóireaċta do ḃí ann.

† "fearann" MS. ‡ "go ngealtóin faoi do ċlú seal" 'san MS, rud naċ dtuigim b'fearr "go músglóċaḋ" 'ná "go músglaiġeaḋ" 'san líne leanas.

Here is a sweet song I got in a manuscript among many Connacht songs, but it is not very like a Connacht song, it is too melodious. I changed the first two lines, for this is how they ran: "*Shee in Vreedyuch tom woot, Dor mutya shee sooarck,*" words which I did not understand. This song was written out very badly, and I only got one copy of it.

THE BREEDYEEN.

'Tis the Breedyeen I love,
All dear ones above,
Like a star from the start*
Round my heart she did move.
Her breast like a dove,
Or the foam in the cove,
With her gold locks apart,
In my heart she put love.

'Tis not Venus, I say,
Who grieved me this day,
But the white one, the bright one,
Who slighted my stay.
For her I shall pray—
I confess it—for aye,
She's my sister, I missed her,
When all men were gay.

To the hills let us go,
Where the raven and crow
In the dark dismal valleys
Croak death-like and low;
By this volume I swear,
O bright cool of fair hair,
That through solitude shrieked
I should seek for thee there.

---

* In singing this, the third line and the seventh line of every verse are often repeated. This metrical version is in the exact metre of the original.

LITERAL TRANSLATION.

It is the Breedyuch I want; The mild woman, gentle, pleasant; The knowledge star of the country, And in my heart she took harbour. Two breasts round and hard, Bright neck like the foam. Fine long yellow hair. And in my heart she took harbour.

It is not Venus of whom I am speaking, Or any other woman of women, But

Teannam go dtí an sliaḃ
Ag éisteaċt leis an ḃfiaċ,
'S na gleanntaiḃ deunaṁ lionn'-duḃ
Mar ar ċailleas mo ċiall.
Ní ḃíonn sólás againn ann
Gan dólás ann a ċeann,
Ní ḃíonn maise gan a masla,
Ná an díreaċ* gan a cam.

'S breáġ a píob mar an aél
A's a brágaid ġealt† gan péin
A's a bán-ċíoċ nár láṁuiġeaḋ
O ġall-ċreaċ‡ go h-éag.
Mo ċeasa trom go h-eug
Mar sgáil duḃ§ ar éun,
'S gur b'í ċráḋ mé le lán-tsoillse—
Fáṫ brig mo sgéil!

Ó'n tráṫ ṫug me gráḋ ḋuit
Ó'n tráṫ ṫug mé gráḋ ḋuit
[Ó'n tráṫ ṫug mé gráḋ ḋuit]
A ḃláṫ na súġ-ċraéḃ
Do ḟáraiġ do ṁéin||
'S ṫug tu gráḋ leat ó'n ngréin,
'S gur ioir do ḋá láiṁ-se
Do b' ḟearr liom dul d'éug.

* "Dreaċ" MS.
† "ċí" 'san MS, rud naċ dtuigim. ‡ "O gal ċreaċ" 'san MS ni ṫuigim é. § "sgail diḃ air can" 'san MS. ni ṫuigim.
|| "Do ḟáraiġ tu an béin," MS.

the brown bright sky-lady, Who is after destroying my heart. I shall not refuse for ever To repeat her name; Sister, I call her, and I conceal it not Beyond all that live of women.

Let us go to the mountain, Listening to the raven, In the black sorrowful valleys, Where the deer speaks; By this book in my hand, O lovely cool of the fair tresses, I would remain with you in solitude, Until the day would waken.

Let us go to the mountain, Listening to the raven In the glens making melancholy, Where I lost my sense; There existeth no joy Without sorrow at its back; There is no beauty without its reproach. And no Straight without its Crooked.

Her throat is fine, like the lime, And her bright neck unpained, And her white breast that was never touched By foreign defeat (?) till death. My heavy

To the hills let us go,
Where the raven and crow
In the dark dismal valleys
Wing silent and slow.
There's no joy in men's fate,
But grief grins in the gate;
Theres no Fair without Foul,
Without Crooked no Straight.

Her neck like the lime
And her breath like the thyme,
And her bosom untroubled
By care or by time.
Like a bird in the night,
At a great blaze of light,
Astounded and wounded
I swoon at her sight.

Since I gave thee my love,
I gave thee my love,
I gave thee my love,
O thou berry so bright;
The sun in her height
Looked on with delight,
And between thy two arms, may
I die on the night.

---

grief till death, Like a dark shadow over a bird; Sure it was she destroyed me with full light—The cause of the substance of my tale.

From the time I gave thee love; From the time I gave thee love; From the time I gave thee love, O Flower of the raspberries, Thy mien overcame, And thou tookest love with thee from the (very) sun, And sure it is between thy two arms I had rather go and die.

My disease (?) and my grief, Without me and thee, my treasure; In dark so rowful glens, Or in a glen of a wood on a bog. It is honestly, gently, decently, I would coax from thee a kiss, O lovely learned star, 'Tis thou art the pick of the young women.

She is a Phœnix, my love, From Helen who took the palm, The gentle accomplished pearl, Of character the most generous of all. O first love of my middle, Do not leave me to death, And sure I would read your accomplishments, In Irish softly.

A's mo ċantal 's mo ḃrón
Gan mé 's tu a stóir
I ngleanntaiḃ duḃa duaiḃreaċa
No i ngleann coille ar móin,
Is cneasta caoin cóir
Do ṁeallfainn uait póg
A réaltain ḃreáġ ṁúinte
'S tu toġa na mban óg.

Is í phoénics mo ġráḋ
O hélen rug bárr,
An péarla ciúin tréiṫeaċ
Is féile ar biṫ cáil,
A ċeud-ṡeirc mo láir
Ná léig mé ċum báis,
'S go léiġfinn-se do ṫréiṫe
i nGaeḋeilg* go sáiṁ.

Ag so rann milis eile, acht mar an t-aḃrán suas, is mó atá blas Muiṁneaċ na blas Connaċtaċ air, ciḋ gur i sgríḃinn Ċonnaċtaiġ fuairear é. Agus ċor leis sin, ní focal Connaċtaċ an focal sin "éisling"=laige, agus is iad na Muiṁniġ go mór-ṁór do ċleaċtaḋ imirt le focal, mar ċiḋmíd ann so. Bheirim an rann ann so le croṫuġaḋ na diċfre atá idir na sean-aḃránaiḃ simpliḋe do ṫug mé ċeana, agus aḃránaiḃ nuaḋa na Muiṁneaċ.

A ṀÁIRE IS TU MO ĠRÁḊ.

A Ṁáire is tu mo ġráḋ, a's gráḋ mo ċroiḋe do ġráḋ
Gráḋ sin gan donas gan éisling,
Gráḋ ó aois go bás, gráḋ ó ḃaois ag fás,
Gráḋ ċuirfiḋ go dlúṫ faoi ċré mé,
Gráḋ gan súil le saoġal, gráḋ gan tnúṫ le spré,
Gráḋ d'fág mé cráiḋte i ndaér-ḃruid,
Gráḋ mo ċroiḋe tar mnáiḃ, 's a saṁuil súd de ġráḋ
Is anaṁ† é le fáġail ag aen-ḟear.

---

* "As Gaolam," MS. † "innuaḋ," 'san MS.

And I would that I were
In the glens of the air,
Or in dark dismal valleys
Where the wildwood is bare;
What a kiss from her there
I should coax without care,
From my star of the morning,
My fairer than fair!

Like a Phœnix of flame,
Or like Helen of fame,
Is the pearl of all pearls
Of girls who came,
And who kindled a flame
In my bosom. Thy name
I shall rhyme thee in Irish,
And heighten thy fame.

Here is a sweet rann I found in another manuscript of mine, but like this song, there is more of a Munster flavour than of a Connacht flavour about it. And besides that, the word *aishling* ("weakness") is not a Connacht term, and it is the Munstermen, too, who used especially to practise playing upon a word, as we see done here. I give the verse to show the difference there is between the old simple songs I have given already, and the newer ones of the Munstermen.

O MAURYA, TAKE MY LOVE.

O Maurya, take my love, love of my heart, thy love,
Love without fear or failing;
Love that *knows* not *death*, love that *grows* with *breath*,
Love that must shortly slay me;
Love that *heeds* not *wealth*, love that *breeds* in *stealth*,
Love that leaves me sorrowing daily;
Love from my heart is *thine*, and such a love as *mine*
Is found not *twice*—but found, is unfailing.*

---

* *Literally.* "O Maurya, thou art my love, and the love of my heart thy love, A love that without pettiness, without weakness, Love from age till death, love from folly growing, Love that shall send me close beneath the clay. Love without a hope of the world, Love without envy of fortune, Love that left me withered in captivity, Love of my heart beyond women, and such a love as that, It is seldom to be got from any man.

Tá an imirt seó leis an bfocal "gráḋ" cosṁúil le imirt i ndán do sgríoḃ an "Mangaire Súgaċ" (Aindrias Mac Craiṫ) o ċondaé Luimniġ. Deir seisean i ndán áluinn do rinne sé ar fonn "Ċailín deas crúiḋte na mbó."

A ċumainn na g-cumann ná tréig mé
'S go bfuilim i n-éag-ċruṫ ad' ḋeóiġ,
A's gur cumann mo ċumainn naċ dtréigfead
A ċumainn go téiḋim faoi an bfód,
O ṫugas duit cumann as géilleaḋ
Mo ċumann-sa a ḟéunaḋ ni cóir,
A's mo ċumann a ċumainn má ṫréigir
Gan cumann ag aén-bean go deó.

Ag so aḃrán eile do ċualaiḋ mé o ṡean ṁnaoi i gCon-na-mara, agus ó ḋaoiniḃ eile. Is aḃrán coitċionn go leór é amearg na ndaoine, agus ċuir mé leis ann so rann no dó do fuair mé i láiṁ-sgríbinn. Do ċualaiḋ mise an sean-bean 'gá ġabáil agus í ag bliġ na mbó, agus do bí tuilleaḋ aici naċ g-cuiṁniġim, agus naċ bfuaireas ó aon duine ó ṡoin.

PEURLA DEAS AN TSLÉIḂE ḂÁIN.

Ceiṫre lá deug gan bréig
Do ċaiṫ mise 'san tsliaḃ
Ag síor-innseaċt mo sgéil
Do béilín ainnir na g-ciaḃ,
Mo ṫaeb le n-a taeb
A's mo ḋá láiṁ tairsti aniar,
Mo beul ar a beul
Gur eulaiġ sin toraınn an ġrian.

Cluinim d'á luaḋ
Agus is caint í ṫuigeas.a lán,
Go dtug mo ċroiḋe gean
Do ṗeurla deas an tSléibe báin,
Gaċ a dtug me d' annsaċt
A's ar ṡanntuiġ me riaṁ de na mnáib
Is í beitiḋ ni h-ainle
M'annsaċt agus mo ġráḋ.

This play upon the word love is like that which the Mong-ir-yah Soogugh—Andrew MacGrath, from the County Limerick—made. He says, in a beautiful poem which he composed to the air of the "Colleen D'yas Crootyee na Mo:"

Oh, love of my love, do not *hate me,*
For love, I am *aching* for thee;
And my love for my love I'll *forsake not,*
O love, till I *fade* like a tree.
Since I gave thee my love I am *failing,*
My love, wilt thou *aid* me to flee?
And my love, O my love, if thou *take not*
—No love for a *maiden* from me.**

Here is another song I heard from an old woman in Connemara, and from others also; it is a rather common song among the people, and I put with it, here, a stanza or two, which I found in a manuscript. I heard the old woman singing it, and she milking the cows, and she had more of it that I do not remember and that I never got from anyone since.

THE PRETTY PEARL OF THE WHITE MOUNTAIN.

Fourteen days, without lie
I spent on the mountain's side,
Ever crying my cry
In the ear of my maiden's pride;
Pleading bitterly,
My side set by her side,
On her mouth my mouth,
Till the sun set southward and died.

I hear it spoken
By many a friendly mouth
How my heart is broken
By her of the White Hill south.
All my affection true
And my hope and my longing at flood,
Are concentred on you,
Maid of O'Hanly's blood.

** *Literally,* "Affection of the affections, forsake me not, And sure I am in a death-condition after thee, And sure the affection of my affection shall I not forsake, O affection, until I go under the soil. Since I gave thee affection and submission, My affection, to deny it is not right, And my affection, O affection,

'S é mo ċreaċ a's mo ḃiṫ
Nac ḃfuil mé mo laċa ḃig ḃáin
Go snáṁfainn go h-aéraċ
I n-eudan na tuile 's na tráġ,'
Ag súil le mac Dé
Go réiḋeóċaiḋ seisean mo ċás
'S go sínfinn mo ṫaéḃ
Le peurla deas an tSléiḃe ḃáin.

Deir siad liom féin
Gur niḋ beag suaraċ an gráḋ,
Aċt is mairg air a mbíonn sé
Mí no seaċtṁain no lá,
I 'nna luiḃe ar a taoiḃ
(Faoi ḋuilleaḃar agus) bláṫ
Agus mé le n-a taoiḃ
Agus craoḃ beag ġlas ann mo láiṁ.

Mo ċreaċ a's mo ḃiṫ
Naċ ḃfuil eudaċ orm ná bláṫ
Ná gearráinín aéraċ
Do ḃeurfaḋ mise aon áit.
Go D'L'acliaṫ na dteurma
Má ṫéiḋim ni ḟillfead go bráṫ
Aċ bíoḋ a roġa féin
Ag peurla deas an tSléiḃ' ḃáin.

Cad é an ṁaiṫ ḃam féin
Dá ndeunfainn capall de bó?
A's cad é an ṁaiṫ ḋam é
Dá ndeunfainn caisleán ar ród?
Cad é an ṁaiṫ ḋam é
Dá ndeunfainn muilionn ar ṁóin?
O ċaill mise an gleus
Le a mbreugfainn ḃeitiḋ mo stór.

---

if thou forsakest—No affection for any woman for ever (for me).

These verses are constructed on different words, one *grau*, the other *cumman*, which sounds better in Irish than any such word-play can in English, since the latter word, for instance, can assume three forms—*cumman*, *humman*, and *gumman*, which keeps up the play without palling on the ear.

This translation is in the metre of the original. *Literally*. Fourteen days without lie, I spent in the mountain. Ever-telling my tale To the little mouth of

'Tis my grief and my pine
    That I'm no white duck on the bay,
On the billows to rise,
    And to dive in the teeth of the spray.
That God may decide on my side,
    And me far away,
And set me beside
    The side of my pearl some day.

They tell me that love
    Is little, "'t is nothing," they say,
But, oh, it's woe for who has it
    A month, a week, or a day.
There she lies on her side
    Gently by light winds fanned,
I sit close to her now
    With a leafy bough in my hand.

Oft I wish I were
    Clothed bright in state like a king,
Or had a winged mare
    To bear me afar on her wing.
To term-keeping Dublin
    If I go I shall fare but ill,
Leaving thee free my girl,
    Thou pearl of the fair White Hill.

What should it profit me
    To make a steed of a cow?
What should it profit me
    To build a castle here now?
What should it profit me
    To build on the meadow a mill,
Since I lost the way
    To bend my fay to my will?

---

the maid of the tresses. My side by her side, And my two hands back across her, My mouth on her mouth Until the sun stole away past us.

I hear it being said, And a talk it is which numbers understand, That my heart gave affection To the Pretty Pearl of the White Mountain, All that I ever gave of affection, Or that I ever coveted of women, She is Betty Nee Hanli, My delight and my love.

'Tis my destruction and my loss That I am not a little white duck Until I should swim airily In the face of the flood and the shore, Hoping for the Son of God That He shall settle my case, And that I might stretch my side By the pretty girl of the white mountain.

Ag so ḋán aisteaċ, agallaṁ no cóṁráḋ—Carmen Amœbæum—idir ṁnaoi agus fear, mar fágmaoid é i bfilíḋeaċt gaċ tíre o aimsir Horatius go h-aimsir Ṫomáis Ui Ṁórḋa, agus mar béiḋ sé coṁ fad a's tá fir agus mná ann. Fuair mé é i litir do sgríoḃ duine éigin go dtí an sean Náisiún nuair bí Tomás Dáibís agus Gaban O Dubṫaiġ 'gá stiúruġaḋ, ag súil, mar is cosṁúil, go g-cuirfidís i g-cló ḋó é. Is fiú a ráḋ ann so go raiḃ leaṫ de na h-Eireannaiġiḃ, ar an laġad, ag labairt Gaeḋeilge 'san am sin, agus gur cuireaḋ mór-ċuid Gaeḋeilge, abráin agus uile ḟórt do'n Náisiún le Gaeḋeilgṫeóraiḃ ar fud na tíre. Is dóiġ go mbeiḋeaḋ siad clóbuailte ann dá mbeiḋeaḋ aon duine ar an bpáipéar d'ḟeudfaḋ a ḋeunaṁ, óir bí Tomás Dáibís an ċapṫanaċ do'n teangaiḃ, act is dóiġ naċ raiḃ aon duine aca leis an gcló do ċeartuġaḋ, agus leis sin is dóiġ naċ raiḃ aon ċló Gaeḋeilge aca. Dubairt an fear do ċuir an dán so ċuca gur mar so do rinneaḋ é. Bí Taḋg O Doirnín, a deir sé—act ní'l fios agam cia an O Doirnín é—ag siúbal tre Eirinn agus ṫáinig sé go teaċ Ui Luinín no Lindon. Bí O Luinín 'nna "biaḋṫaċ," is é sin fear a raiḃ teaċ osgailte aige ag tabairt biḋ agus dídinn i n-aisge do luċt-siúbalta na sliġe. Ċuaiḋ O Doirnín asteaċ agus tar éis na seire no an tsuipeir, do cuireaḋ cláirseaċ ann a láiṁ, mar buḋ gnáṫaċ ann san tír 'san am sin, le feicsint ar ṁian leis ceól do ḋeunaṁ. Ni raiḃ eólas ag aon duine 'san tiġ ar O Doirnín, agus bí iongantas mór orra nuair ṫosaiġ sé an ceól buḋ binne ar biṫ do ṫarraingt ó'n g-cláirsiġ. Ċuir sé sin eud ar ḋeirbḟiúr Ui Luinín óir do bí si féin 'nna rig-ċláirseóir. Dubairt sí naċ raiḃ aon ḟear do ċuaiḋ an tsliġe sin le fada d'ḟeudfaḋ ceól mar sin do ḋeunaṁ, agus tar éis cóṁráiḋ ḟada leis, ċuir sí dúbḟlán faoi, an ċláirseaċ do ḟeinm 'nna h-aġaiḋ féin, agus muinntir an tiġe ag éisteaċt leó mar breiṫeaṁaiḃ. Ṫosaiġ Taḋg O Doirnín agus ċum se a's ḟeinn sé an leaṫ-rann so ar an móimid, ex tempore as a inntinn féin, agus d'ḟreagair sise é ann san móḋ agus 'san miosúr ceudna.

TAḊG AGUS MAIRE.

Taḋg: Buḋ ċiúin an tráṫ, bí tulċa i mbláṫ
Nuair ċonnairc mé tu a Ṁáire,
Máire: Níor breáġa an lá 'ná ṫusa, an tráṫ
Do bain tu a Ṫaiḋg an báire.

They say to myself That love is a small petty thing, But it's woe for whom it is on, A month, or a week, or a day. Lying on her side Beneath the foliage and blossoms, And I by her side And a little green bough in my hand, etc.

The remaining verses present no difficulty and need not be translated.

Here is a curious poem, a dialogue or discourse—Carmen Amœbæum—between a man and a woman, as we find it in the poetry of every country from the time of Horace to that of Tumaus O'Moore, and as it will be while men and women exist. I found it in a letter which some one wrote to the old *Nation* at the time when Thomas Davis and Gavan O'Duffy were steering it, hoping, as is likely, that they would put it in print for him. It is worth mentioning here that about half of the Irish, at the least, at this time spoke Gaelic, and that a good deal of Irish songs and different things were sent to the *Nation* by "Iresians" throughout the country. No doubt they would have been printed had there been anyone on the staff of the paper able to do so, for Thomas Davis was very friendly to the language; but it is likely they had no person to correct the proofs, and, besides that, had probably no Irish type at this time.

The man who sent them this poem said that it was composed in this way. Teig O'Dornin, he says—but I do not know what O'Dornin—was travelling through Erin, and came to the house O'Luneen or Lindon. Lindon was a Beetagh or hospitaller; that is, one who kept open house, giving food and shelter gratis to those who went that way. O'Dornin went in, and after the repast or supper, a harp was placed in his hand, as was customary in the country at that time, to see if he wished to make music. Nobody in the house knew O'Dornin, and there was great wonderment on them when he began to draw from the harp the sweetest music at all. That made Lindon's sister jealous, for she was herself a queen harpist. She said that there was no man went by that way for a long time was able to make music like that, and after a long conversation with him she challenged him to play the harp against herself, and the people of the house listening to them as judges. Teig O'Dornin began, and on the moment composed and played this half stanza extempore, and she answered him in the same way, and the same metre.

TEIG AND MARY.

TEIG: Bright was the air, the hills were fair,
When first I saw thee, Mary.
MAURYA: Not brighter they than thou, the day
Thou tookest Teig the "bairy."*

---

*The Anglo-Irish for a "goal" in hurling, from the Irish *báire.*

This translation is exactly in the metre of the original. *Literally* :—
T.—Calm was the time, hills were in blossom, when I beheld thee, Mary.
M.—Not finer was the day than thou wert, the time thou tookest Teig the

Taḋg : Do rosca, a spéir, ar ḋaṫ an aeir,
'S má 's féidir é níos áille,
Máire : Ní'l aer ná (g)leann is fios dam ann
Níos sgíoṁaiġe 'ná do ċáil-se.

Taḋg : Buḋ ḋuibe bí an ġrian ag luiḋe
Ioná do ġnúis a Ṁáire,
Máire : An reult no 'n ġrian ní ṫaiḋḃriġeann trian
Oireaḋ soluis le do sgáil-se.

Taḋg : Ar an tsluaġ ban-siḋe buḋ ṁaiṫ 's buḋ ġnaoi
Do ġnúis ġeal-ċaoiṁ a Ṁáire,
Máire : Is fearr i ngné sluaġ siḋe 'ná mé,
Aċt b'ḟearr do ġné-se an trá sin.

Taḋg : Bárr-sgéiṁ an ġráḋ i d'ċuaċan breáġ*
Do ċonnairc mé ort a Ṁáire,
Máire : Is tusa d'ḟiġ an cuaċan mín
Le míne† ċaoin do ġáire.

Taḋg : Do rosca caoiṁ'‡ do ḋealḃuiġ an ḟiġe
Do ġaḃ mo ċroiḋe-se a Ṁáire,
Máire : Is ort-sa tá an ball-seirc do ġnáṫ
A lasas gráḋ gaċ stáidbean.

Taḋg : Má 's áil leat mé a ġráḋ mo ċléiḃ
Is leat go h-eug mé a Ṁáire,
Máire : Táid lasraċ' cluain 'gam' ċráḋ go ciúin,
Uċ! úṁluiġim duit, ciḋ náireaċ.

Ní fios dúinn cad é is deireaḋ do'n sgeul-so, no ar úṁlaiġ an óigbean dó dá rírib, no an ag magaḋ faoi do bí sí.

---

* "Bárrsgéiṁ an graigh mar cucacan braigh," 'san MS.

† Ní léir dam cad é an focal so ann san MS. is cosṁúil le "miniḋeaċt" é. ‡ "caoi" 'san MS.

---

goal. *T.*—Thy eyes, O sky-lady, of the colour of the air, and, if possible, more lovely. *M.*—There is no air or valley (?) that I know of, more beautiful than thy reputation. *T.*—Blacker is the sun when setting than thy features, Mary. *M.*—Neither star nor sun exhibit one-third as much light as thy shadow. *T.*—It were a good and a comeliness for the host of the fairy women (To have) thy bright gentle countenance, Mary. *M.*—Better is the fairy host in appearance than I, but better thy appearance at that time (than theirs). *T.*—Top-beauty of love in thy fine curls I beheld upon thee, Mary. *M.*—It is thou who wovest the smooth curl? with the gentle softness of thy laugh. *T.*—Thy gentle eyes have shaped the web which took my heart, O Mary. *M.*—It is on thee is ever the love-spot which kindles the love of every stately woman. *T.*—If I am pleasing to

TEIG: Thy eyes are bright as stars of night,
Each one God's candle-bearer.
MAURYA: There is no star of all that are,
But thou by far art fairer.

TEIG: The setting sun shows black and dun,
And cold, beside thee, Mary.
MAURYA: There is no sun of all that run
To which I could compare thee.

TEIG: The fairy host might make their boast
Of thy sweet features, Mary.
MAURYA: More fair they are than I, by far,
But thou more fair than fairy.

TEIG: Top-knots of love all else above,
Lurk in thy tresses, Mary.
MAURYA: Thou hast a smile which must beguile,
So gay it is, so airy.

TEIG: Thy bright eyes spin a net so thin,
Thou took'st me in it, Mary.
MAURYA: A love-spot thou hast on thy brow,
Of charms it is not chary.

TEIG: Thy slave I'll be; thou sees't in me
Thy thrall and lover, Mary.
MAURYA: No longer free, I yield to thee,
All shamefaced, all unwary."

We do not know what is the end of this story, and whether the lady submitted to him in reality, or whether it was jesting at him she was.*

---

thee, O love of my bosom, I am thine till death, Mary. *M.*—There are treacherous flames silently destroying me. Alas, I submit to thee, although shamefaced.

* There was a celebrated poet O'Dornin, born near Cashel in 1682, who lived most of his life in Armagh. But his name was Peadar (Padder), not Teig, and his wife's name Rose, not Mary. The gentleman who sent this piece to the *Nation*, accompanied it with a poetic version by a "talented friend" of his own, each half verse of which—regardless of any reminiscence of Cowper—ended in "My Mary," to which the second half of the verse as invariably responded with the delightful assonance of "My Thady." Of course, this is not in the Irish, where the lady's difficulty was to find a fitting extempore rhyme for her own name, Maurya.

Déarfaiḋ mé anois píosa atá le fáġail ann s gaċ áit ar fud na tíre, Bean an Ḟir Ruaiḋ. Ní'l ḟios agam cad fáṫ ar ċuir na daoine an oiread sin spéis ann san abrán so munab é an fonn atá air. Ni ḟeicim féin mórán ceóil ná filiḋeaċta 'sna foclaib, aċt tá an giota so ċoṁ deaġ-aiṫniġṫe sin, ṫeas agus ṫuaiḋ, naċ dtig liom a ḟágbáil amuiġ. Fuair cara ḋam féin na briaṫra leanas o ḃeul ṡeanduine i g-condaé na Gaillime, agus fuair mise uaiḋ-sean iad. Fágaim amaċ rann no dó naċ bfuil ro ṡoiléir.

Bean an Ḟir Ruaiḋ.

Tá siad d'á ráḋ
    Gur tu sáilín socair i mbróig
Tá siad d'á ráḋ
    Gur tu béilín tana na bpóg.
Tá siad d'á ráḋ
    A ṁíle gráḋ go dtug tu ḋam cúl,
Ciḋ go bfuil fear le fáġail
    'S leis an táilliúr bean an Ḟir Ruaiḋ.

Do ṫugas naoi mí
    I bpríosún, ceangailte cruaiḋ,
Boltaiḋ ar mo ċaolaib
    Agus míle glas as súd suas,
Ṫabarfainn-se siḋe
    Mar ṫabarfaḋ eala cois cuain,
Le fonn do ḃeiṫ sínte
    Síos le bean an Ḟir Ruaiḋ.

Ṡaoil mise a ċeud-ṡearc
    Go mbeiḋ' aon tiġeas idir mé 's tu
Ṡaoil mé 'nna ḋéiġ-sin
    Go mbreuġfá mo leanb ar do ġlúin.
Mallaċt Ríġ Neiṁe
    Ar an té sin bain ḋíom-sa mo ċlú,
Sin, agus uile go léir
    Luċt bréiġe ċuir idir mé 's ṫu.

I shall now give a piece which is to be found in every place throughout the country—the Red Man's Wife. I do not know why the people took such pleasure in this song, unless it is the air which is on it. I do not see myself much music or poetry in the words, but this piece is so well known North and South that I cannot omit it. A friend of mine got the words which follow from an old man in the County Galway, and I got them from him. I leave out a verse or two which are not very clear.

THE RED MAN'S WIFE.

'Tis what they say,
  Thy little heel fits in a shoe.
'Tis what they say,
  Thy little mouth kisses well, too.
'Tis what they say,
  Thousand loves that you leave me to rue;
That the tailor went the way
  That the wife of the Red man knew.

Nine months did I spend
  In a prison closed tightly and bound;
Bolts on my smalls*
  And a thousand locks frowning around;
But o'er the tide
  I would leap with the leap of a swan,
Could I once set my side
  By the bride of the Red-haired man.

I thought, O my life,
  That one house between us love would be;
And I thought I would find
  You once coaxing my child on your knee;
But now the curse of the High One
  On him let it be,
And on all of the band of the liars
  Who put silence between you and me.

---

* There are three "smalls," the wrists, elbows, and ankles. In Irish romantic literature we often meet with mention of men being bound "with the binding of the three smalls."

Tá crann ann san ngáirdín
  Air a bhfásann duilleaḃar a's bláṫ buiḋe,
An uair leagaim mo láṁ air
  Is láidir nach mbriseann mo ċroiḋe;
'S é sólás go bás
  A's é d'ḟágail o ḟlaiṫeas anuas
Aon ṗóigin aṁáin,
  A's é d'ḟágail o Ḃean an Ḟir Ruaiḋ.

Aċt go dtig lá an tsaoġail
  'Nna reubfar cnuic agus cuain,
Tiucfaiḋ smúit ar an ngréin
  'S béiḋ na neullta ċoṁ duḃ leis an ngual
Béiḋ an fairrge tirm
  A's tiocfaiḋ na brónṫa 's na truaiġ'
'S béiḋ an táilliúr ag sgreadach
  An lá sin faoi Ḃean an Ḟir Ruaiḋ.

Do ċuir Eireannach éigin beagán mí ó ṡoin, cóip eile de'n abhrán so i gclóḃ, dó bí sgríoḃṫa, deir se, níos mó 'ná ceud bliaḋain ó ṡoin i gcondaé na Miḋe. Clóḃuail sé i bpáipéar Albannach é, "Na hImsiriḋe Óbain." Ag so cuid dé.

Bean an Ḟir Ruaiḋ. Cóip eile.

'Sé do beaṫa ann san tír-se
  A ḟaoilinn is deise faoi ġruaiḋ
'Ná an bean do bí siar
  Ag Naois Mac Uisneach 'san g-cuan.
Sgriosfaiḋ mé an tír
  Anios go h-imeall Ros-cuain,
'S an uair casfad arís
  Béiḋead claoiḋte ag Bean an Ḟir Ruaiḋ.

There grows a tree in the garden
  With blossoms that tremble and shake,
I lay my hand on its bark
  And I feel that my heart must break.
On one wish alone
  My soul through the long months ran,
One little kiss
  From the wife of the Red-haired man.

But the Day of Doom shall come,
  And hills and harbours be rent;
A mist shall fall on the sun
  From the dark clouds heavily sent;
The sea shall be dry,
  And earth under mourning and ban;
Then loud shall he cry
  For the wife of the Red-haired man.*

Some Irishman, a few months since, printed another copy of this song, which he says was written down more than a hundred years ago in the County Meath. He printed it in a Scotch paper, the *Oban Times.*† Here is some of it:

THE RED MAN'S WIFE.

(Another copy).

Salutation to thee into this country
  O seagull more lovely in countenance
Than the woman in the West whom
  Naesi, son of Usneach, had in the harbour.
I shall destroy the country
  Down to the border of Roscuain,
And when I turn back again
  I shall (myself) be overthrown by the Red man's wife.

---

*This translation is in the curious broken metre of the original. *Literally*: They are saying it, That thou art the quiet little heel in a shoe. They are saying it, That thou art the thin little mouth of the kisses. They are saying it, Thousand loves, that thou hast turned thy back on me, Though a man may be had. The tailor's is the wife of the Red man, etc. The other verses offer no difficulty. There is no mention of a tailor in the older copy. It may have been altered to suit local circumstances.

† Or rather, the well-known and humorous Gaelic *littérateur* who writes under the name of Fionn (Mr. Henry Whyte) published it, but some Irishman, I think, gave it to him.

Is gile do ḃráġaid
 A ṁíle gráḋ ná eala ar tuinn,
Is deirge do ġruaḋ
 'Ná an rós do ṫig ar na crainn,
Is binne do ḃeól
 'Ná 'n ċuaċ 's í seinm go binn
'S gur míne 'ná 'n síoda
 Gaċ dlaoi d'á dtig ar do ċeann.

A ḃruinnioll gan smál
 A ḃfuil an dealraḋ deas ar do ġruaḋ,
Cia bé an t-óġánaċ bán
 Do b'áil liom leat-sa do luaḋ;
Cia ċeilim ar aon
 An t-áḋḃar fá ḃfuilim faoi ġruaim (?)
Dá mbeiḋinn gonnta ag an éag
 'S í mo cheud ġráḋ bean an ḟir Ruaiḋ.

A ḃláṫ-bean na sgéiṁe
 Cuirim ceud míle beannaċt leat uaim,
Tá mé gonnta ag an éug
 I n-éugmais do ṫáṫaiġṫe gaċ uair,
Dá mb'eól dam bean ḃreugaḋ
 Ċuirfinn i g-céill duit m' anacra cruaiṫ
'S má ḟillim go h-eug
 'Sí mo ċeud fearc bean an ḟir Ruaiḋ.

Dá mbeiḋinn 'san tír ḟíos
 I bpriosún ceangailte cruaiḋ
Boltaiḋ ar mo ċuim
 A's míle glas ar súḋ suas.
Ṫaḃarfainn-se sgrib
 Mar do ṫaḃarfaḋ eala cois cuain
D'ḟonn a ḃeiṫ sínte
 Seal oiḋċe le bean an ḟir Ruaiḋ.

Whiter is thy neck
  Thousand loves, than the swan on the waves,
Redder is thy cheek
  Than the rose which comes on the trees.
Sweeter is thy mouth
  Than the cuckoo, and she singing sweetly,
And sure smoother than the silk
  Is each lock which grows upon thy head.

O damsel without spot,
  Who hast the pretty gloss upon thy cheek.
Whoever the fair-haired youth is
  I would like to betroth to thee,*
Why (?) conceal I it on anyone
  The reason why I am under gloom?
Though I were wounded by the death
  My first love is the Red man's wife.

O blossom-woman of the beauty,
  I send with thee a hundred thousand blessings from me,
I am wounded by the death
  In lack of thy society every hour.
If I knew how to coax a woman,
  I would explain to thee my hard calamity.
And if I return for ever
  My first-love is the Red man's wife.

If I were in the Down country
  In prison bound hard,
Bolts on my waist,
  And a thousand locks from that up;
I would give a flight
  As a swan would beside a harbour,
With pleasure to be stretched
  For the while of a night by the wife of the Red-haired man.

---

* I do not well understand the third, fourth, and fifth lines; perhaps cíɑ is meant for chá which is used instead of ní "not" in parts of Meath.

Ag so abrán maiṫ fuair me ann mo ṡean-sgríbinn féin agus ni ḟacaiḋ mé i n-aon áit eile é.

Bríġid Óg na g-Ciabh.

Cuirim do ċuimrigiḋ*
Ar Ḋia ['gur impíḋim]
Réiḋtiġ ḋam an bealaċ agus ná fulaing mé i bpian
Dá dtiucfá-sa fá an tsliaḃ
'N áit a gcóṁnaiġeann an fiaċ
[Ag] déanaṁ lionnduiḃ fá na gleanntaiḃ 's gur leat ċaill mé mo ċiall.

Tá gráḋ agam ar ṁnaoi
Agus ċráḋ sí mo ċroiḋe,
Ruḃ binne liom í naoi n-uaire 'ná an ċuaċ ar an g-craoiḃ,
'S 'ná lon-duḃ an ḃéil ḃuiḋe
'S an ceirseaċ† le n-a ṫaoiḃ
'S í‡ an smóilín binn breugaċ do ġéar-loisg mo ċroiḋe.

An g-cualaiḋ siḃ-se trácht
Ar ċluanaiġeacht na mná?
Is ar feabas do sgríoḃfaḋ sí le caol-ṗeann ar ċlár,
Ní'l sé le fáġail
Ann 'san ḃFrainc ná 'san Spáin
Naċ ḃfuil díol fir mar ċéile innti, péurla an ċúil ḃáin.

Ġeoḃainn-se go leór
Luċt síoda 'gus sróil,
Ḣataiḋ míne duba, agus fáinniḋe buiḋe óir,
Ni raċaiḋ mise leó§
Aċt riot-sa, a ṁíle stór,
A rúin-ċeart iarla Anntruim 's gur tu plannda de'n ḟuil ṁóir.

---

*=coimirce, "cuirim ṫu faoi ċoimirce .i. sgáṫ, Dé," b'éidir.
† "is a ceassaċ" 'san MS. ‡ "Sna," MS.
§ "Ni leó raċuinn" 'san MS. "riot-sa" 'san líne leanas=leat-sa.

Here is a good song I found in my own old manuscript, one which I have never met anywhere else—

YOUNG BREED OF THE TRESSES.

Unto God I pray
Every night and day
Not to leave me pining, but to speed me on my way ;
Oh, come my love to-day
Where the ravens seek their prey,
We shall sorrow in the valley where you set my heart astray.

For gone it is and strayed,
My love is on a maid,
I think her nine times sweeter than the cuckoo in the glade,
Or, thrush, within the shade,
Or blackbird when he played
His sweetest notes to cheer us, and my soul is dismayed.

Oh, have you heard them say
How arch and bright and gay
Is my lady, how she writes with a pen in her play ?
There is not, so they say,
In France or Spain to-day,
A man who would not leap to take the hand of my may.

Girls I'd get, I swear,
Who silk and satins wear,
Hats both dark and glossy, and rings rich and rare ;
But see, I leave them there,
Thou only art my care,
Sister of Antrim's Earldom, so fragrant and so fair.

---

* This translation is in the metre of the original. *Literally* :—

I put to his guardianship Upon God, and I request, Smooth for me the way and do not suffer me (to be) in pain. If thou wert to come with me under the mountains, Where the raven dwells, Making melancholy through the valleys, and with you I have lost my senses.

I have love for a woman, And she ruined my heart. I thought her nine times sweeter than the cuckoo on the branch Or the blackbird of the yellow mouth, And the song-finch (?) at his side. She is the melodious coaxing little thrush that bitter-burned my heart, etc.

The next verses offer no difficulty and need not be translated. "Díol fir" in the third verse, means "a sufficiency for any husband;" that is, one good enough to satisfy the most exacting.

Ag so abrán maiṫ eile fuair me i n-America. Ann san g-ceud rann tá an cailín ag ráḋ naċ leigfiḋ sí do'n ḃuaċaill a meallaḋ, agus ann sna trí rannaiḃ leanas tá an buaċaill ag cur a ċáis i g-céill dí agus 'g á ḃreugaḋ.

MÓR NÁ BEAG.

[An cailín ag labairt].

Mór ná beag níor luaiḋeaḋ riaṁ mise
  I mbuaiḋreaḋ fir ná céile,
A's go ḃfuair mé mo ḃeaṫa ariaṁ gan aiṫis,
  Ní mó* gur baineaḋ lasaḋ as m' éadan.
Má 's é dioġḃáil mo ċarad ṫug sliġe duit ar mo ṁeallaḋ
  Ná d'aon ḟear d'a ḃfuil beó i n-Éirinn
A's má tá tusa ag braṫ mise do ċur ó raṫ
  Cuirim Críost tá ar neaṁ 'nna ḋéiġ ort.

[Eisean ag iarraiḋ í do ḃreugaḋ].

Goirim tu a ṡiúir, goirim ṫu a rúin,
  Goirim ṫu naoi n-uaire,
Goirim do ċúl tá trioplaċ [dlúṫ],
  A's goirim do ċum seang uasal.
Goirim ṫu a ġráḋ, tá m'anam ar do láiṁ,
  Taraiġ,† ṫusa, trá agus fuasgail,
Congḃaiġ mé ó'n éug agus bíḋim agad féin,
  A ḃruinnioll na ngeug nglan uasal.

Tá baċ agam ar ṡliaḃ a's níl aon duine 'nna ndiaiġ
  A's mise do m' ċiaraḋ leó-san,
A's m'ḟocal duit a Ḋia ó's ort atá mo ṫriall
  Gur baineadar mo ċiall go mór díom,
Mise beiṫ liom féin folaṁ, oċ ni ḃéiḋead,
  Anois agus mé i dtús m'óige,
A's gur mall guṫ gaċ éin a labras leis féin ‡
  Ar ṁala no ar ṡliaḃ móinte.

---

* "mór," 'san MS. † = "tar." ‡ Tá an líne seó i n-abrán eile, is sean-ḟocal é.

Here is another good song which I got in America. In the first verse the girl is saying that she will not let the boy deceive her, and in the three stanzas that follow, the boy is explaining his case to her and persuading her.

GREAT OR SMALL.

Great or small, no word was ever spoken
Betrothing me to another.
My fame has been fair, and my life without care,
I have no blush of shame I must smother.
If my friends being few, prompts an ill thought in you,
Or in any man else who has seen us,
And who hopes he may lead me to shame and to need,
I put Christ and His cross between us.

[HE ANSWERS].

I call on thee, my love ; I call on thee my dove ;
I call on thee nine times over ;
I call on thy cool, so tressy and so full,
And I call on thy form as a lover.
I call thee through the land, my soul is on thy hand,
Then leave me not banned and in trouble ;
Save me from the death, O maiden with the breath
And the limbs of a freeborn noble.

Upon the mountain side my kine are running wide,
They have not a guide to herd them.
I left them there, God knows, to seek for my wild rose ;
My thoughts like waves arose since you stirred them.
Alone, why must I be, with none to go with me?
I shall draw from my youth as a fountain :
For every bird, you know, who sings alone, sings slow
On the side of the grove or mountain.

This translation is in the metre of the original. *Literally* :—
Great or small was I never betrothed In trouble of husband or consort, And sure I found my life ever without reproach, And more (than that), no blush was ever struck from my face. If it was the loss of my friends gave you a way to betray me, Or any other man alive in Erin, And if you are intending to put me from prosperity, I set Christ who is in Heaven to avenge it on you (*literally*, "after it upon you")
I call thee, O sister, I call thee O secret-love, I call thee nine times, I call thy cool that is clustering and close, And I call thy form slender, noble. I call thee O love, My soul is on thy hand, Come thou for awhile and relieve me. Keep me from the death, and let me be thy own, O damsel of the limbs clean (shaped) and noble, etc.

Tá lasaḋ ann san ngréin agus lonraḋa dá réir
    Timċioll do ḃéilín ṁóḋṁair,
A's gur follus do'n tsaéġail gur ṁearaiġ tu le céill
    Tuilleaḋ agus dá ċeud óig-ḟear.
A ainnir ḃreáġ ġeal ḟéiṁ na bfad-ḟolt cuaċ[aċ] claon
    Lasann mar an scuaiḋ (?) ómra
'S gur b'é d'iarrfainn-se de ṁaoin no de ṡaiḋḃreas an tsaoġail
    Cead sínte leat gaċ aon oiḋċe Dóṁnaiġ.

Tá rann eile ann san aḃrán so ṫosaiġeas, "A ċúil áluinn ḋeas" mar tá sé i n-"Éamon an Ċnuic," agus is follusaċ é go raiḃ dá aḃrán measgṫa le ċéile ann so, mar ċonncamar é deunta go minic. Tá an dá rann ṫosaiġeas "Goirim ṫu a ṡiúr" ann san "Mall Duḃ an ġleanna" mar an g-ceudna.

Ann san aḃrán so leanas tá an cailín ag caoineaḋ tar éis í do ḃeiṫ tréigṫe le n-a gráḋ. Is simpliḋe agus is binn an ċeasaċt atá sí ag deunaṁ. Saṁluiġeann sí a múirnín le "reult tríd an g-ceó," ráḋ ċuireas ann ár g-cuiṁne an dán breáġ sin i leaḃar Uí h-Argadáin, an dán is breáġa de na dántaiḃ, b'éidir, atá 'san ríġ-leaḃar sin

"Ċonnairc mé ag teaċt ċugam í tre lár an tsléiḃe
    Mar reultan tríd an g-ceó."

CAILÍN DEAS AN ĠLEANNA.

A óganaiġ óig mar reultan tríd an g-ceó
    Do ṫugas-sa mo ġean go léir* duit,
A's do ġeall tu ḃeiṫ róṁam ag coill ġlais na g-cnó
    Go g-cuirfimís ár g-cóṁairle i n-éinḟeaċt.
Tuig a ṁíle stór naċ bfuil peacaḋ ar biṫ ċoṁ mór
    Is measa agus is mó le deunaṁ
Ná maiġdean ḋeas óg do ṁeallaḋ le (do) ṗóig
    Agus feallaḋ uirri go deó 'nna ḋéiġ sin.

This "I call thee" is a word often used when things or people display any unaccountable restlessness; the full form is, "I call and consecrate you to myself," and it is used against fairy agency. Ciapaḋ in the following verse means "torturing," and mearaiġ means to "set astray." "Every bird who sings by himself sings slow" is, I think, a proverb.

---

* "mór" san MS.

A flame comes from the sun when day is almost done,
I see it on thy small mouth staying;
For you have set in play—as all men know to-day—
Hundreds of young men straying;
O maiden of the hair so fair beyond compare,
On the air like an amber shower,
This world has, I swear, no wealth that can compare
With but one kiss there in thy bower.

There is another verse in this song which begins *A Hool awlin yass*, as it is in the song of "Ned of the Hill," and it is evident that there are two songs mixed up here, as we have seen done frequently. The two verses which begin *Guryim hoo a h'yewr*, "I call thee, O Sister," are also in the song of "Dark Moll of the Valley."

In the song which follows, the girl is lamenting after her being forsaken by her love. The complaint which she makes is simple and melodious. She likens her sweetheart to a "star in a mist," a saying which calls to our recollection that fine poem in Hardiman's book, perhaps, the finest of all the poems that are in that king-book—

"I saw her come towards me through the middle of the mountain
As a star shines through the mist."

OH, YOUTH WHOM I HAVE KISSED.

Oh, youth whom I have kissed, like a star through the mist,
I have given thee this heart altogether,
And you promised me to be at the greenwood for me
Until we took counsel together;
But know, my love, though late, that no sin is so great
For which the angels hate the deceiver,
As first to steal the bliss of a maiden with a kiss,
To deceive her after this and to leave her.

A Radaiġe (?) o a rúin an aitreaċ leat go buan
    Mar ċuir tu le buaiḋreaḋ an tsaoġail mé (?)
'S gur ċuir tu do ḋúil i n-airgiod 's i mbuaiḃ
    Agus i seasaideaḃaiḃ duḃa an tsléiḃe.
B'ḟearr liom go mór beiṫ ar taoiḃ buaċaill óig*
    'Ná sealbán bó ar taéḃ ċnuic
'S é d'imeóraḋ (liom) air ṗean (?) agus cluiċċe cruaiḋ na ngeall
    Agus siúbalfaḋ an saoġal go réiḋ liom.

Ag dul 'nna luiḋe do'n ngréin, mo ċreaċ, mo ḋiṫ go geur!
    Is mise bíos i bpéin an uair sin,
Go mbuḋ saṁuil do m'ġné an té sínead ann san gcré,
    'S a Ṁic Ṁuire naċ mór an truaġ† sin!
Mo ċáirde uile go léir, an ċuid aca nár eug
    Gur ṫugadar geur-ḟuaṫ dam,
Gan d'ḟocal ann a mbeul, aċt "ó ṁill tu ṫu féin
    Fulaing do réir sin buaiḋreaḋ."

I n-aḃrán eile atá agam "Cuaiċín Beinne Éidir" naċ dtugaim ann so, atá fear ag deunaṁ na casaoide ceudna i dtaoiḃ ṁná, agus mar duḃairt an cailín go mb'ḟearr léiṫe buaċaill óg 'ná "sealḃ bó ar ṫaoiḃ ċnuic," deir seisean

B'ḟearr liom cailín óg
    Ag córuġaḋ mo leaptan
'Ná saiḋḃreas ríġ na Fóḋla
    'S mo ṗósaḋ le cailliġ.

Ní'l mórán filiḋeaċta ann san aḃrán so agus ní aḃrán Connaċtaċ é agus sin é an t-áḋḃar faoi a bfáġaim amaċ é, aċt is fiú a ṫabairt fá deara go ndearnaḋ é 'san am ann a raiḃ Gaeḋeilg ag na daoiniḃ i m Beinn-Éidir, seaċt míle o Ḃ'l'áṫcliaṫ.

* "seasaṁ buaċ la óig" san MS. rud naċ dtuigim.
† "sgeul" 'san MS.

This translation is in the metre of the original. *Literally.* O young youth, like a star through the mist I have given thee my love completely, And you promised to be before me at the greenwood of the nuts Until we would put our counsels together. Understand, O thousand treasures, that there is no sin so great, Worse and greater to do, Than to deceive a pretty young maiden with your kiss And betray her for ever afterwards.

O Rody (?), O secret love, dost thou constantly repent How thou hast sent me on the world's trouble, And how thou hast set thy affection on money and on kine And on black heifers of the mountain? I should greatly sooner be at the side of

And do you now repent for leaving me down bent
    With the trouble of the world going through me,
Preferring sheep and kine and silver of the mine
    And the black mountain heifers to me?
I would sooner win a youth to love me in his truth
    Than the riches that you, love, have chosen,
Who would come to me and play by my side every day
    With a young heart gay and unfrozen.

But when the sun goes round I sink upon the ground,
    I feel my bitter wound at that hour;
All pallid, full of gloom, like one from out a tomb,
    O Mary's Son, without power.
And all my friends not dead are casting at my head
    Reproaches at my own sad undoing,
And this is what they say, "since yourself went astray,
    Go and suffer so to-day in your ruin."

In another song which I have, called "The Cuckoo of Bin-édar," which I do not give here, there is a man making the same complaint about a woman, and just as the girl said that she preferred a young boy to the "possession of cows on a hill-side," so he says—

I had sooner a young girl
    Preparing my couch
Than the wealth of the King of Fola (Ireland),
    And my marriage with a hag.

There is not much poetry in the song, and it is not a Connacht one, hence I omit it, but it is worth observing that it was made at a time when the people of Binédar (the Hill of Howth), six miles from Dublin, spoke Irish.

---

a young bohal Than (have) possession of cows on the side of a hill. It is he who would play with me on *pan* (?) and (play) the hard game of the pledges, And who would freely walk the world with me.

On the sun's going to lie down—my destruction, my loss, grievously—It is I was in pain at that hour, And the likeness of my countenance was that of him who was stretched in the clay, And O Son of Mary, is not that the great pity! My friends, all of them entirely, as many of them as did not die, Ah, they have given me bitter-hatred, Without a word in their mouths but, "Since you have ruined yourself, Now suffer trouble according."

So aḃrán eile ann a ḋtráċtar ar Ḃeinn Éidir.

Neilliḋ na gCocán.

'S a Ḋia gan mé am' iasgaire
 Ṡoir i mBeinn Éidir,
Agus Neilliḋ na g-cocán
 Ḃeiṫ i g-ceart-lár Loċa Éirne
Raċfainn-se os síoll
 Síos ar fad d'á feuċain,
'S ní ṫiubḃrainn brob luaċra
 Ar ṁnáiḃ uaisle na h-Éireann.

'S a Neilliḋ, Ḋia ḋílis!
 Ní cubaiḋ* ḋuit beiṫ am' ṫréigean,
'S gur a n-aice do ṁín-ċnis
 Buḋ ṁian liom beiṫ ad' ḃreugan.
Mo láṁ ar an mBíobla
 'S mé ṡíos ar mo ġlúnaiḃ,
Naċ sgarfainn leat ċoiḋċe
 Go sínfiḋe 'san úir mé.

Tá cóifrín deas buiḋe agam
 'S é líonta le criostal,
'S tá glas geur go riġin air
 'S é go fíreannaċ curṫa.
Aċċuingim ar Íosa
 A's ar Ríġ Ċolam Cille
A ṁaiġdean gan mí-ġreann
 Deaġ-ċríoċ ort ó Ṁuire.

Agus b'éidir go mbéiḋinn-se
 Agus maiġdean an ċúil ómra
Ar maidin ag éisteaċt
 Le h-aifrionn ár bpósta;
Munab cúis a ráċfas,
 Ar a h-aġaiḋ í, béiḋead brónaċ
Mar na lon-duḃ' ar na coillṫiḃ
 Le soillse an tráṫnóna.

---

*=ní cóir é, ní oireaṁnaċ é. Labairṫear an focal so mar "caoi" no "cuíḋe." Tá se an ċoitċionn i n-áiteaċaiḃ i g-Cúige Múṁan.

Here is another song in which mention is made of Binédar.

NELLY OF THE TOP KNOTS.

Dear God ! were I fisher and
Back in Binédar,
And Nelly a fish who
Would swim in the bay there,
I would privately set there
My net there to catch her,
In Erin no maiden
Is able to match her.

And Nelly, dear God !
Why ! you should not thus flee me,
I'd long to be near thee
And hear thee and see thee.
My hand on the Bible
And I swearing and kneeling
And giving thee part
Of the heart you are stealing.

I've a fair yellow casket
And it fastened with crystal,
And the lock opens not
To the shot of a pistol.
To Jesus I pray
And to Colomkill's Master,
That Mary may guide thee
Aside from disaster.

We may be, O maiden,
Whom none may disparage ;
Some morning a-hearing
The sweet mass of marriage,
But if fate be against us,
To rend us and push us,
I shall mourn as the blackbird
At eve in the bushes.

'S a Ḋia gan mé ar linn (?) léiṫe
'S gan uimpi aċt a léine,
No i bPáris na Fraince
No ar inris Loc' Éirne,
Ag cur fíos mo ċainte
'S ag deiṁniuġaḋ mo sgéil dí,
Mar súil go mbeiḋinn-se agad
A ṁaiġdean na gcraéḃ-folt.

Ag so abrán do rinne O Cearḃalláin, do réir mo láiṁ-sgríbinne-se, aċt ní ṁeasaim féin gur b'é. Is dóiġ go raiḃ a lán abrán sgríoḃṫa ar an bfonn ceudna, agus ní'l aon aṁras orm naċ bfuil an port agus an t-abrán níos sine 'ná aimsir Uí Ċearḃalláin. Ḃeir Seáġan O Dálaiġ—fear naċ bfuair ariaṁ a ṡáiṫ molta ar son an ṁéid do rinne sé i g-cúis na n-abrán Muiṁneaċ—píosa ḋúinn air a nglaoḋann sé "Bean Duḃ an Ġleanna," agus tá cuid dé an cosṁúil leis an dán so. Deir seisean gur b'é Éamon an Ċnuic O Riain do rinne an t-abrán atá ann a leaḃar féin timċioll na bliaḋna 1730-40. Tá an fonn simpliḋe agus an-ḃinn. Ag so mar fuair mise é.

MALL DUBH AN ĠLEANNA.

Is ag Mall Duḃ an ġleanna
Tá mo ġráḋ-sa i dtaisge,
Is í naċ bfuair guṫ ná náire,
Is caoiḋeaṁail múinte maiseaċ
Duḃairt sí liom ar maidin
Imṫiġ a's ná feuċ go bráṫ mé.
Ní'l óganaċ deas
O Ṁúṁain go Tuaim 's go Gaillim,
Ná ó sin go Laiġniḃ Uí h-Eaġra,
Naċ bfuil triall ċum an ġleanna
Ar eaċraiḃ slíocaiḋ sleaṁain,
(Ag) feiṫeaṁ ar an mbean duḃ is áille.

---

* This is in the metre of the original. *Literally*:—

NELLY OF THE TOP-KNOTS.

I wish to God that I were a fisher* West in Benedar, And Nelly of the top-knots To be in the middle of Lough Erne. I would go privately Down all the way to look at her, And I would not give the point (?) of a rush For the (other) gentle women of Ireland.

* Literally, "O God! without me in my fisher.

Oh, God, were she with me
Where the gull flits and tern,
Or in Paris the smiling,
Or an isle in Loch Erne,
I would coax her so well,
I would tell her my story,
And talk till I won her
My sunshine of glory.

Here is another song, which, according to my manuscript, Carolan composed, but I do do not think myself that it was he. Probably there were a number of songs written to the same old air, and I have no doubt that both air and song are older than Carolan's time. Shawn O'Daly—a man who never received sufficient praise for all he did for the Munster songs—gives us a piece which he calls "Ban Dhuv in Glanna," *i.e.*, "The Dark Woman of the Valley," and part of it is very like this poem. He says that it was Éamon, or Ned of the Hill, O'Ryan, who composed the song which is in his book about the year 1730-40. The air is simple and very sweet. Here is how I found it:—

DARK MOLL OF THE VALLEY.

My heart loves to dally
With Dark Moll of the valley,
No blame nor shame she had ever;
How gently, not scorning,
She bade me in the morning
To go, and return to her never.
There is no handsome youth
From the lands of the south
Unto Galway's old city of story,
But on hunters sleek they rally
In hundreds to the valley,
To see the Dark Girl in her glory.

And O Nelly, Oh, dear God, It is not proper for thee to be forsaking me, And sure it was beside thy white skin I had desired to be coaxing thee, My hand on the Bible And I down on my knees, That I would never part with thee Until I should be stretched in clay.

I have a nice little yellow casket And it filled with crystal, And I have a sharp lock toughly on it And it truly placed; I implore Jesus And the king of Columkille, O maiden without ill favour, A good end on thee from Mary.

The remaining verses offer no difficulty, and do not need translation

Dá bfáġainn-se bean ó'n bPrionnsaċ,
A's bean ó'n Luinnseaċ,
Agus bean eile ó Ríġ Seórsa,
Inġean Ċoirnéill Dingam
A's í do ḃeiṫ le fonn liom,
No bean eile agus míle bó léiṫ,
Inġean óg an Iarla
A's í do ḃeiṫ go priaċlaċ
D'á m'iarraiḋ féin le pósaḋ,
Mná deas' an doṁain
Dá bfaġainn orra mo roġan
Is Mall Duḃ an Ġleanna ṫóġfainn.

Gairim ṫu a ṡiúir,
Gairim tu a rúin,
Agus gairim ṫu naoi n-uaire,
Gairim-se do ċúl
Tá feamuinneaċ breáġ dlúṫ,
A's gairim-se do ċom deas uasal.
Gairim-se arís ṫu a ġráḋ,
Tá m'anam ar do láiṁ,
Muna dtigiḋ tusa, tráṫ, agus fuasgailt,
Cosain mise ó'n éag
Feasta a ċoiḋċ' ḋuit féin,
A ainnir ċaoin na g-céadfa ró-ḋeas.

Tá branndaiġ agus beóir
Ar ċeart-lár an róid,
Agus cláiréad ar an nós céudna,
Bantraċt ban óg
Le siúḃal leat ann san ród,
Sin a's dul i g-cóiste sé n-eaċ.
Geoḃair sioda agus sról
(Ag) sileaḋ leat go feóir,
Cáṫaoir agus bórd-eudain,
A's naċ fearr sin a stóir,
Agus eulóġaḋ liom a stóir,
'Ná cóṁnuiḋe faoi brón i n-Éirinn.

---

* This translation is in the exact metre of the original. *Literally* :—
It is with Dark Moll of the valley My heart is laid up in keeping. It is she got neither blame nor shame, It is courteously, mannerly, beautifully, She said to me in the morning, Go and see me not for ever. There is no handsome youth

Were a maid of the Frenches,
A maid of the Lynches
Or of George's maidens to take us;
Or Colonel Bingham's daughter
To love me as I taught her,
Or one with thousands of acres.
Or could I get the girl
The daughter of the Earl
In her robes of pearl to marry,
Of all the women fair
To take my choice of there,
I would choose the Dark Girl of the Valley.

I call thee a-roon
I call thee right soon,
And I call on thee nine times over,
I call on thy cool,
Like sea-weed fine and full,
And thy noble shape, as a lover;
I call thee through the land
My soul is on thy hand,
Then leave me not banned and forsaken,
Save me from the death
And keep me for thyself
Most beautiful, most tender maiden.

There's brandy amply stowed
On the middle of the road
And the claret is not put into hiding,
And maidens bright as day
To take thee on thy way,
And a carriage and six to ride in.
Satin you will get
And silk, and golden fret,
And a throne and a royal faring;
And were it not, my dear,
Far better than be here,
Under grief, under fear, in Érin.*

From Munster to Tuam and Galway Or from that to Leyny of the O'Hara But is journeying and drawing On sleek smooth steeds Attending upon the most beautiful Dark Woman.

If I were to get a wife from the French, And a wife from the Lynch, And another

Ni ṫig liom aon rud do b'ḟeárr ḋéanaṁ ann so 'ná an dá ḃéarsa i n-abrán Ui Ḋálaiġ atá cosṁúil le dá ḃéarsa i m'abrán-sa do ċur síos ann so, ag taisbéant na caoi ann a n-aṫruiġeann na sean-abráin seó ó ċúige go cúige. Tá an dá abrán éagsaṁail ar fad ó ċéile, aċt aṁáin 'san dá ḃéarsa so. Ag so mar fuair O Dálaiġ iad; ní aṫruiġim-se a ṁóḋ-sgriobṫa-san.

Ní'l ógánaċ cailce
O Ḃ'l'acliaṫ go Gailliṁ,
Ná as sin go Tuama Ui Ṁeara,
Naċ ḃfuil ag triall 's ag tarraing
Ar eaċaiḃ donna deasa,
Ag tnúiṫ leis an mbean Duḃ áluinn.
Ġeaḃainn-se bean 'sa' Múṁan,
Triúr bean i Laiġean,
Agus bean o riġ geal Seórsa,
Bean na lúbaḋ buiḋe
D'ḟáisgioċ mé le na croiḋe,
Bean agus dá ṁile bó léi,
Inġion óg an iarlaḋ
Atá go tein dubaċ diacraċ
Ag iarraiḃ mise d'ḟáġail le pósaḋ,
'S dá ḃfáġainn-se féin mo roġa
De ṁná deasa an domain
Is í an Ḃean Duḃ ó'n nGleann do b'ḟearr liom.

Is sompla maiṫ é seó ar áḋḃar na n-aṫruġaḋ ṫigeas ann sna sean-abránaiḃ. Ċiḋmid mar d'aṫraiġ an Muiṁneaċ é do réir inntinne a ċúige féin ag cur ainm' na n-áit sin ar a .raiḃ eólas aige féin, ann san abrán; agus mar do rinne an Connaċtaċ an rud ceudna ag traċt ar ṁnáiḃ uaisle do ḃain le muinntiriḃ do ḃí cliúṫaċ ar feaḋ Connaċta go léir, mar atá na Prionnsaiḃ agus na Luinnsiġ, no na Fríonnsaiḋ agus Loingsiġ mar sgríobṫar iad mar an g-céadna. Ar an áḋḃar so ni ṁeasaim go raiḃ láṁ ar biṫ ag an g-Cearḃailánaċ ann san abrán so muna b'é gur ċuir sé béarsa no dó eile leis, ag tógḃáil seompa nuaiḋ ar an tsean ċloċ-ḃonn.

---

wife from King George, The daughter of Colonel Bingham And she to be with gladness with me, Or another wife and a thousand cows with her. The young daughter of the Earl, And she to be eager Seeking for myself to marry, The fair women of the world If I were to get of them my choice It is Dark Moll of the Valley I would take, etc.

I cannot do anything better than put down here the two verses in O'Daly's song, which are like two verses in my one; thus showing the way in which these old songs change from province to province. The two songs are altogether different from one another, except in these two verses. Here is how O'Daly found them. I do not change his orthography. Mangan has translated these lines thus:—

Not a youth from Dublin town
Unto Galway of renown,
    Or thence to Toomevara, but is laden,
On steeds bounding free
With love-gifts to thee,
    My loveliest, my dark own maiden.
In Momonia I could find
Many damsels to my mind,
    And in Leinster—nay, England, a many;
One from Georgy, without art
Who would clasp me to her heart
    And a beauty is the lass among many.
The daughter of the earl,
Who walks in silks and pearl,
    Would fain have me netted in her thrall yet.
But could I have my choice,
How much could I rejoice
    To wed thee, my dark maiden of all yet.

This is a good example of the cause of the changes which come in these old songs. We see how the Mweenugh (Munster man) changed it according to the spirit of his own province, putting in the song the names of those places which he knew himself, and how the Connacht man did the same thing, speaking of ladies who belonged to families renowned through all Connacht like the Frenches and Lynches. For this reason, I do not think that Carolan had any hand in this song, unless it were that he added a verse or two to it, raising a new chamber on the old foundation.

"*Feamuinneach*" in the third verse means "clustering like sea-weed," a word often applied to hair, and *bord-eudainn* in the last verse means, I think, a "sideboard," or some piece of furniture. Carolan uses the word. *Gairim* in the third verse is also spelled *goirim* as in the song "Great or Small," where the verse has been already translated.

Aċt atá cóip eile agam sgríobṫa le Dóṁnall Mac Consaidín ar ċondaé an Chláir, atá cosṁúil le cóip Uí Ḋálaiġ, aċt ní'l sí ċoṁ cosṁúil léiṫe naċ fiú a taḃairt ann so, óir buḋ ċóir an méad cóip agus is féidir de na príoṁ-aḃránaiḃ ainmneaṁla so do ċruinninġaḋ agus do ċur i g-cló. Ní'l an dán so sgríobṫa ann sna líntiḃ gearra ann a ḃfuil dán Uí Ḋálaiġ, aċt ċiofiḋ an léiġṫeóir ar an móimid gur ann san miosúr céudna iad.

Pol Dubh an Ghleanna.

Atá bó agam ar ḟliaḃ, is fada mé 'nna diaiġ a's do ċaill mé mo
ċiall le nóḃċar.
D'á seólaḋ soir (a's) siar, a's gaċ áit a ngaḃann an ġrian, no go
ḃ'filleann sí aniar ('san) tráṫnóna.
Nuair féaċaim-se anúnn* 'san mbaile a ḃfuil mo rún tuiteann ó
mo ṡúil ġlais deóra
A Ḋia ṁóir na ngrás tabair ḟuasgailt ar mo ċás a's gur bean
Dub a d'ḟág fá brón mé.

Cia bé ċiḋfeaḋ mo ṫeaċ 's gan de ḃíon air aċt seasg, 's é déanta
ar ṫaoiḃ an ḃóṫair,
Go dtagann an beaċ, a's go ndéanann an nead le grian agus le
teas an ḟóġṁair,
Nuair críonann an tslat ní fanann uirri meas, mar ḃíonn ar an
mbuinne is óige,
'S a ċúil áluinn deas a dtug mo ċroiḋe ḋuit gean, cuirim slán
agus céad go deó leat.

Do ġeaḃainn bean Muiṁneaċ, do ġeaḃainn bean Laiġneaċ, do
ġeaḃainn bean agus dá ṁíle bó léi.'
'S i bean na ḃfáinniḋe buiḋe an ḃean do ċráḋ mo ċroiḋe, no bean
eile as an tír-se Ṡeóirse.
Atá inġean ag an iarla a's tá sí go diacraċ ag iarraiḋ mise
d'ḟáġail le pósaḋ,
A's dá ḃfáġainn-se mo roġa de ṁnáiḃ deasa an doṁain is í Pol
Duḃ an Ġleanna b'ḟearr liom.

---

*="anonn," foirm Ṁuiṁneaċ.

---

* This translation is in the metre of the original. *Literally*:—
I have a cow upon a mountain and I am a long time after her, And I have lost my sense through a consort. Driving her (the cow) east and west, and wherever the sun goes Until she returns back in the evening. When I look over there to the village where my sweetheart (roon) is, Tears fall from my grey eye,

But I have another copy of this song, written by Donal Considine, or the county Clare, which is like O'Daly's copy, but not so like it that it is not worth while to give it here, for it were well to collect and print as many copies as possible of these renowned prime songs. This poem is not written in the short lines in which O'Daly's poem is, but the reader will see on the spot they are in the same measure.

THE DARK GIRL OF THE VALLEY.

Upon the mountain brow I herd a lowing cow,
(And my sense is gone now through a maiden);
I drive her east and west, and where'er the sun shines best,
To return with her white milk laden.
But when I look above, to the village of my love,
My grey eyes fill in their dreaming;
O mighty God of grace, take pity in my case,
'Tis the Dark Girl left them streaming.

Whoever saw my house, with no roof but the rush,
Where the road bends out to the far west,
The bee loves to roam and to build there his home
In the sun and the heat of harvest.
When withered is the root, the bough will bear no fruit
'Tis the young twigs shoot by the river,
O lovely golden fay, who stole my heart away,
Farewell to thee to-day, and for ever.

I would get in Leinster a wife, or in Munster,
Whose thousand-cow dowry all paid is
(The maiden of fair hair has left me in despair),
Or a lady of King George's ladies.
The Earl has a daughter, excess of love has brought her
With me to trifle and to dally,
My choice if I could find of the women of mankind
I should choose the Dark Girl of the Valley.

O great God of grace, give a relief for my case, And sure it is the Dark Woman has left me under grief.

Whoever would see my house with no roof on it but sedge, And it made upon the side of the road, Sure the bee comes and makes the nest With the sun and heat of harvest. When the rod withers there remains on it no fruit As there be's upon the youngest sprout, And O beautiful, handsome cool, to which my heart has given love, I send with thee forever a farewell and a hundred.

The third verse presents no difficulty.

She is the Dark Poll of the valley, she is the Dark Poll, the best, She is the Dark Poll the brightest and finest, Her throat like the swan, her face like the

'Sí Pol Duḃ an Ġleanna, 'sí Pol Duḃ do b'ḟearra, 'sí Pol Duḃ buḋ ġile breáġṫa í,
A píb mar an eala, a h-éadan mar ṡneaċta, 's a com seang singil áluinn.
A dá láiṁín Ṁuire, na g-cúig méara fuinte, do ḟíolraiġ ó'n maiġre ṁánla,
Nuair ġabann an eala amaċ cailleann an ġrian a teas, agus úṁluiġeann an ġealaċ le gráḋ ḋí.

Ċiḋmid mar do glacaḋ an t-abrán so le fear boċt agus le fear saiḋbir le seinm d'á múirníniḃ, fear aca ag iarraiḋ an ṁaigdean do ḃreugaḋ leis as Éirinn go dtí an Ḟrainc no an Spáin, agus 'gá gealladh bainnis ann a mbeiḋeaḋ an brannḋaiġ agus an fíon ċoṁ h-iomadaṁail sin go mbeiḋeaḋ siad le n-ól ar ċeart-lár an ḃóṫair, agus ag gealladh cóiste sé gcapall do'n ṁnaoi le cuideaċt ban-óg. Aċt ní'l ag an donán eile aċt aon ḃó ar ḟliaḃ agus bo-ṫáinín gan aon ċúṁdaċ air aċt seasg no luaċra. Is follusaċ mar sin do réir mo ḃaraṁla-sa go raiḃ an fonn sin agus cuid de na briaṫraiḃ sean go leór, agus gur aṫruiġeaḋ iad féin mar d'iom-caireaḋ iad o áit go h-áit agus ó ċúige go cúige le daoiniḃ do ċuir ḃéarsaiḋ nuaḋa leó—ḃéarsaiḋ do ḃain le n-a g-cás nó le n-a g-cineaṁain féin.

Ag so abrán eile an tsimplíḋe, obair duine tuaiṫe gan aṁras, ann a g-cuireann an duine boċt a ḃrón i n-úmal le fíor-ċuma. Is follusaċ ó'n abrán go ndeaċaiḃ se go b'l'aċliaṫ ag iarraiḋ a leasa, agus gur ṁarḃ an t-aṫruġaḋ é. Bhí sé ag fáġail báis, mar is cosṁúil, nuair rinne sé an píosa so. B'éidir gur b'é com-ráid ḃó, do ruġ a-ḃaile leis é go cúige Connaċt. No b'éidir gur ḟill sé féin tar éis a ṫinnis. Cia inneósas dúinn anois é!

GRÁḊ MO ĊROIḊE ṪU.

Gráḋ mo ċroiḋe ṫu a Ḃriġdín ṁaerḋa,
Is minic 'san oiḋċe a smuainim féin ort,
Tá mise tinn, ní'l mo léiġeas ag aon neaċ
A's brón ar an ngaoiṫ naċ dtugann dúinn sgeula.

---

snow, And her waist slender single(?) handsome. Her two Mary's little hands *(I do not understand this)* of the five kneaded fingers, Which were propagated from the gracious maiden, When the swan goes out the sun loses her heat, And the moon submits with love to her.

Observe the curious and typically Gaelic "anacolouthon" in the beginning of the second verse, where the antecedent clause "whoever would see my house" is left un-

Dark Girl of the Valley, Dark Girl that is lovely,
Dark Girl that is radiant and tender,
Her throat and her brow like the swan on the snow
And her shapely form so slender.
Her hands shaped aright, with fingers soft white
That Mary gave from above to her,
When my swan leaves her seat the sun loses his heat,
And the moon does obeisance with love to her.*

We see how this song was taken both by a poor man and a wealthy one to sing to their sweethearts, a man of them seeking to coax the maiden with him out of Erin to France or Spain, and promising her a wedding at which brandy and wine would be so plenty that they would be to be drunk on the middle of the road, and promising the lady a coach with six horses and a company of young women. But the other poor wretch has nothing but one cow upon a mountain, and a little hut with no thatch on it but sedge or rushes. It is evident then, in my opinion, that the air and some of the words are old enough, and that they were altered according as they were carried from place to place, or from province to province, by people who added new verses to them—verses which concerned their own case or their own fate.

Here is another very simple song, the work, no doubt, of some peasant, in which the poor man expresses his grief with real melancholy. It is evident from the song that he went to Dublin to seek his luck, and that the change killed him. He was dying, apparently, when he composed this piece. Perhaps it was a comrade of his who brought it home with him to Connacht; or, perhaps, he returned himself in spite of his illness. Who can tell us?

STAR OF MY SIGHT.

Star of my sight, you gentle Breedyeen,
Often at night I am sick and grieving;
I am ill, I know it, and no deceiving,
And grief on the wind blows no relieving.

---

finished without any relative. The idea in the poet's mind appears to have been that his love should marry while yet young, as the bee makes its nest in the sunshine and as the twig blossoms in its youth. Instances of these elliptical half-expressed thoughts are very common in these songs.

Twelve hundred years before this, St. Columcille also had written of the Súil ghlas, *or "grey eye," looking with regret at vanishing Erin. It is curious to find his very words repeated here.*

Má ġabann tu an bealaċ so siar, no an bóiṫrín,
Beir mo ḃeannaċt mar a ḃfuil mo stóirín,
Dá mbeiḋinn 'nna h-aice ḃeursainn póg ḋi
Aċt nuair naċ ḃfuilim silim deóra.

Ċuir mé litir ann san ḃposta
Mar a ḃfuil mo ṡearc, go raiḃ me tuirseaċ,
'Sé dubairt sí liom go mbuḋ ḃeag an doċar
'S an té ḃíos i ngráḋ go mbíonn a inntinn corruiġṫe.

Beir mo ḃeannaċt go bonn Ṡléiḃ Beaċla
Mar éiriġeann grian 's mar luiġeann an ġealaċ,
Tá ceó liaṫ ar ḃ'L'acliaṫ na mallaċt
'S ní léar ḋam an t-aer os mo ċeann ná an talaṁ.

Brón ar an mbás is gránna an niḋ é,
Ṡaoil mé riaṁ go meallfaḋ bríob é,
Ḃeursainn dó Éire lán faoi ċaoraiḃ
Aċt mé leigean do Loċ-Riabaċ ag feuċain mo ġaolta.

Is fada liom uaim na bóiṫre móra
'S gan fiú na mbonn faoi mo ḃrógaiḃ
Ciḋ go dtéiḋim ċum an aifrinn ní le deḃótion,
Aċt le súil, O, go ḃfeicfinn mo ṁíle stór ann.

A Ḃaile-caṫ-riabaċ, mo ċúma, ceud slán leat
'S iomḋa lá breáġ aoibinn do ċaiṫ mé láiṁ leat,
Ag síor-ól fíona 's mo ṁian ar láiṁ liom
Ḃíḋinn gan piġin 's bíḋeaḋ m'inntinn sásta.

Tá na beursaiḃ sin níos simplíḋe 'ná na cinn eile seó. Ní ṫugaim aċt dá rann de'n abrán so.

---

* This translation is in the simple metre of the original. In most of the verses, but not all, there are one or two interlineal vowel rhymes.

Literally. Love of my heart thou art, courteous Breedyeen, It is often in the night myself thinks of you; I am ill, and no one has my cure, And grief on the wind that brings us no tidings.

If you go that way, westwards (O wind) or by the boreen, Bring my blessing to where my storeen is; If I were near her I should give to her a kiss, But since I am not I shed tears.

I put a letter into the post (to) Where my darling is (saying) that I was tired; 'Twas what she said to me that the loss was small, And that he who is in love his mind be's moved.

O wind, if passing by that far boreen,
Blow my blessing unto my storeen;
Were I on the spot I should hear her calling,
But I am not, and my tears are falling.

Into the post I put a letter,
Telling my love that I was no better;
Small the loss, was her answer to me,
A lover's mind should be always gloomy.

Wind, greet that mountain where she I prize is
When the gold moon sets and the white sun rises;
A grey fog hangs over cursèd Dublin,
It fills my lungs and my heart it's troubling.

Ochone for the Death, when the breath is going!
I thought to bribe it with bumpers flowing;
I'd give what men see from yonder steeple
To be in Loughrea and amongst my people.

Och, the long high-roads I shall never travel!
Worn my brogues are, with stones and gravel;
Though I went to mass, there was no devotion
But to see her pass with her swan-like motion.

Farewell Loughrea, and a long farewell to you;
Many's the pleasant day I spent in you,
Drinking with friends, and my love beside me,
I little dreamt then of what should betide me.*

Those verses are simpler than these others. I only give two verses of this song.

Bring my blessing (wind?) to the foot of Slieve Beachla, Where the sun rises and the moon sets; There is a grey fog over Dublin of the curses, And the air over my head is not visible to me nor is the ground.

Grief on the Death! it is an ugly thing, I always thought that a bribe would deceive it. I would give to it Erin full up of sheep But only it to let me (go) to Loughrea to behold my kindred.

I think it long from me the high-roads are, Without as much as the soles under my brogues. Though I go to Mass 'tis not with devotion, But hoping, Oh, that I might see there my thousand treasures.

O Bally-ca-reawugh, my grief, a hundred farewells to you, Many's the fine pleasant day I spent beside you! Ever drinking wine and my desire at my hand (*i.e.*, my dear beside me). I used to be without a penny, and my mind used to be satisfied.

An Ṁóḋaṁuil Ṁaiseaċ.

'Sé mo ċráḋ a's mo ṁilleaḋ gan mo ġráḋ agus mise
'S an Spáin no a ḃfad ó ár ngaoltaiḃ,
I n-árus coille cois tráiġ' no toinne
'S gan neaċ 'san g-cruinne 'nn ár ngaor ann,
Is dlúṫ do ḋruidfinn le plúr na g-cumann
'S is ceannsa ṗógfainn a béilín,
Ċóireóċainn dí leabaiḋ a's luiḋfinn 'nna h-aici
A's ṫabairfinn-se tamall d'á breugaḋ.

Ar an Ṁóḋaṁuil Ṁaiseaċ is meaḃar liom labairt
'S ar a tréiṫiḃ ḃí measarḋa múinte,
Sgríoḃfad go fairsing de ḃrigh gur cailleaḋ
Na mílte pearsa ḃí ag súil lé,'
Tá ceud fear aca-san beó d'á maireann díoḃ
I bpéin i nglasaiḃ ag Cúpid,
'S ní saor tá mise aċt mo ṁoġ i ndaor-ḃruid dí
'S is baoġal go g-cuirfiḋ sí 'múġ' mé.

I ndeire an aḃráin seó deir an file, no b'éidir file eile ag deunaṁ magaiḋ faoi n-a ḃoċtanas féin agus é ag iarraiḋ cailín mar í.

Súd an spré do ġearrfainn dam féin leis an ainḟir
Dúiṫċ' eile trasna, 's Cionn-tsáile
(A) ḃfuil o Ṡliaḃ go Sionnainn 's dá dtrian Ḋún gceannaing
'S a ḃfuil siar ó ḋeas go Portláirge.
I Múṁan leat raċfainn, Dúrlas do ġearrfainn duit,
Agus Cluain-geal-meala ċum áitriḃ,
'S ḃeiḋ' do ċóistiḋe ar lasaḋ le h-ór buiḋe-ḋearg
'S fir óga ag feiṫeaṁ go lá ort.

Is cuiṁin liom dán eile de'n tsórt so do rinne file i g-conndaé an Chláir ag roinnt amaċ an ċonndaé sin ar a luċt-ṁuinntearais aṁuil agus dá mbuḋ úḋaċt do ḃí sé ag deunaṁ, agus an duine boċt gan troiġe talṁan aige féin, aċt ag deunaṁ magaiḋ faoi a easḃuiḋ maoine.

---

* This translation is in the metre of the original. *Literally :—*
It is my destruction and spoiling, without my love, and me (to be) In Spain or far away from our kin, In the dwelling of a wood beside shore or wave, And without a person in the world in our vicinity. It is closely I would approach to the flower of the affections, And it is mildly I would kiss her little mouth. I would arrange for her a couch and would repose near her. And I would give a while to coaxing her.

THE MANNERLY HANDSOME ONE.

'Tis my pain, I'm not going through waves overflowing,
To Spain with my love to take service,
Or seeking a home by the sea and the foam,
Or in woods where none could disturb us;
It's close I would come to my beautiful one,
I would teach her that true love a bliss is,
I would build her a couch that would face to the south
And steal from her mouth its kisses.

Of my beautiful fair, with whom none can compare,
I would speak till I fairly tired,
And long would I write of her beauty so bright
By which youths were mightily fired;
Of how many have died for her fairness and pride,
And all have been tied by Cupid,
And I am a slave on the brink of the grave,
And my heart is hopeless and stupid.*

At the end of this song the poet says—or, perhaps, some other poet mocking at his own poverty, and him to be seeking a girl like her—

This is the fortune which I would cut out for myself with the girl,
The estate of Éile (the O'Caroll's territory?) across, and Kinsale,
All that is from Slieve to Shannon and two-thirds of Dungannon,
And all that is south-west to Waterford;
I would go into Munster with you, I would cut out Thurles for you,
And bright Clonmel for a habitation,
And your couches should be shining with yellow-red gold
And young men attending on thee till day.

I remember another song of this sort which a poet in the County Clare composed, dividing out that county to his friends as though he were making a will, and the poor man without a foot of ground to himself, but mocking at his own lack of wealth.

Of the Mannerly Handsome one I desire(?) to speak And of her accomplishments that were moderate, I shall write widely (of them), because there have been lost The thousands of persons who hoped for her. There are of these a hundred men (yet) alive who still survive of them (put) in pain, and in locks (fetters) by Cupid, And I am not free (either) but a bondsman in unfree bondage, And there is a danger that she shall put me astray.

So dá rann eile ar ainḟir óig. Ní'l fios agam cad é is ciall de'n ráḋ gur ḃuaḋaiġ sí (.i. rug buaiḋ) ar Ríġ Seumas. B'éidir go raiḃ sí ag an g-cúirt, agus "go dtáinig an sgeul ṫar tráiġ anios" go raiḃ an Ríġ féin i ngráḋ léiṫe.

Úna Ṗeucaċ.

A Úna ṗeucaċ rug buaiḋ ar Ḃénus
A's 'dḟuadaiġ an sgéiṁ ó ṁnáiḃ an tsaoġail
A stuaḋ na féile ar ṡnuaḋ na gréine
Do ġluais gan ḃréig o Ṗárrṫas naoṁ.
A ainḟir ṁúinte ḃeusaċ do ḃuaḋaiġ* ar Ríġ Seumas
Is luaiḋte an sgeul ṫar tráiġ anios,
Naċ truaġ leat mé gan suan i d' ḋéiġ-se
A ġruaiḋ mar ċaor 's an bainne tríd.

Gaċ dlaoiġ mar an t-ór léiṫe síos go bróig
Leis an ḃfaoileán ṁóḋṁar ṁánla ṁín
Maoṫ-ċroḃ ró-ġlan, mar ċum Críost, dar ndóiġ †
'S gaċ siolla d'á glór mar ċláirseaċ ċaoin.
A ċiall na Fóḋla, a ṁian na n-óig-ḟear
Sgaoil an brón tá i lár mo ċroiḋe,
Mo ṗian tá mór muna ḃfáġainn aċt póg
Ó n-a grís-ḃeul róis ḃeiḋinn slán arís.

Tar éis an aḃráin-gráḋ do "Úna Ṗeucaċ" tigeaḋ ceann eile de'n ċineál ceudna do "Ḃrigid Ḃeusaċ," tarraingim é as mo ṡean láiṁ-sgríbinn féin, aċt ċonnairc mé, ni ċuiṁnigim cia an áit, dá ċóip eile dé.

Ḃriġid Ḃeusaċ.

Ṗósfainn-se Ḃriġid Ḃeusaċ
Gan cóta bróig ná léine,
A stóir mo ċroiḋe dá mb'féidir
Liom, do ṫroisgfinn duit naoi dtráṫ,

* "a ḃuaḋ" 'san MS. † "ar ndóiṫe" MS.

* This translation is in the metre of the original. There is double vowel rhyme in most of the uneven lines, running over into the even ones.

Literally. O Showy Una, who carried off victory from Venus, And plundered their beauty from (all) the women of the world, O arch (?) of generosity of the appearance of the sun, Who voyaged without lie from holy Paradise; O maiden, learned, mannerly, who overcame King James, The story is repeated down across

Here are two other ranns to a young maiden. I do not know what is the meaning of saying that she overcame King James. Perhaps she was at court and "the story came down across the strand" that the King himself was in love with her.

SHOWY UNA.

My Una, a queen is, more true than Venus,
For who that seen is, can thus entice,
You brightest arch in the white sun's march,
You lighten hearts out of Paradise;
You overcame King Shamus, your name it was so famous,
The story came to us down the stream.
You stole my rest and my soul from my breast
O cheek like the berry when mixed with cream.

Each curl like the gold in a furling fold,
On my girlish soaring sea-bird flung,
Her palm so white, that Christ shaped aright,
And the tone of her voice is a harp well strung;
O daughter of fame, is it all in vain?
Call this flame from my deep heart's core,
My hope is this—if I win one kiss
From her rose-flame lip I shall sigh no more.*

After the love song to "Showy Una" another of the same sort to "Courteous Breed" may come. I extract this song from my own manuscript, but I have seen, though I do not remember where, two other copies of it.

COURTEOUS BREED.

Though shoeless, shirtless, grieving,
Foodless, too, my Breedyeen,
Surely I'll not leave you,
Nine meals I'll fast for you.

---

shore, Do you not think it a pity me (to be) without rest after you, O countenance like the berry and the milk through it.

Every curl like the gold with her, down to her shoe, With the sea-mew courteous, gentle, smooth, Soft palm very clean, as Christ shaped it certainly, And every syllable of her voice like a gentle harp. O sense (?) of Fola (Erin), O desire of the young men, Loose this pain which is in the midst of my heart, My pain is great; If I did not get but a kiss From her ember-mouth of rose I should be whole again.

Gan ḃiaḋ gan deoċ gan aon ċuid
Ar oileán i Loċ Éirne,
D'ḟonn mé a's tu ḃeiṫ i n-éinḟeaċt
        Go réiġfimís ár g-cás.
A ġruaiḋ ar ḋaṫ na gcaor-ċon
A ċuaiċín ḃáirr an tsléiḃe,
Do ġeallaḋ ná deun breugaċ
        Aċt éiriġ (roiṁ an lá)
'S i n-aiṁḋeóin * dliġe na cléire
Go dtoġfainn ṫu mar ċéile,
'S a Ḋé, nár ḋeas an sgeul sin
        Duine ag eulóġ' le n-a ġráḋ.

Ġeit mo ċroiḋe le buaiḋreaḋ
Agus sgannraiġ mé naoi n-uaire
An ṁaidin úd do ċualaiḃ mé
        Naċ raiḃ tu rómam le fáġail,
'S a liaċt lá faoi ḟuairceas
Ċaiṫ mise 's tu i n-uaigneas
'S gan neaċ ar biṫ d'ár g-cúṁdaċ
        Aċt an "iug" a's é ar an gclár.
Dá ḃfáġainn amaċ do ṫuarasg
Dá dtéiḋfeá go bonn cruaiċe
Raċfaḋ an sgéul ro ċruaiḋ orm
        No leanfainn do mo ġráḋ,
'S go mb'ḟearr (liom) sínte suas leat
'S gan fúinn aċt fraoċ a's luaċair
Na (ḃeiṫ) 'g éisteaċt leis na cuaċaiḃ
        Ḃíos ar siúḃal ag éiriġe lá (i.e. laé).

'S é áḋḃar m'osna 's m'éagcaoin
Gaċ maidin ṁoċ d'á n-éiriġim
A ċúil na lúb 's na bpeurla
        Naċ tu ḃí dam i ndán,
'S ní iarrfainn-se de ḟéirín
Aċt mé a's tu ḃeiṫ i n-éinḟeaċt
I n-áit icéint† 'nn ár n-aonar
        Go leagfainn ort mo láṁ.

---

* "Ingḋeóin" san MS. Laḃairṫear mar sin é i meaḋon Connaċta.
† Laḃairṫear "éigin" mar "icéint" i gConnaċtaiḃ agus mar "éigint" i Muṁan.

Upon Loch Erne's islands,
No food, no drink beside me,
Still hoping I may find you,
My childeen, to be true.
O cheek, so blush-abounding,
O berry of the mountain,
Your promise, love, is sounding
For ever in my ear.
And spite of cleric's frowning
I'd take you as I found you;
It's I who would go bounding,
Eloping with my dear.

I frightened in my heart, for
It leapt nine times and started,
That morning that you parted
And were not to be found.
And all the happy evenings
I spent beside my dearest,
And no one came between us,
And the jug was on the ground.
I'll travel through the island
Still seeking for your tidings,
And hard it will betide me
If I find not my love.
I'd sooner sit beside you
On rushes through the night time,
Than listen to the finest
Of the birds of the grove.

The reason of my sighing
Each morning of my rising,
Is you to be a-hiding
And lost from sight of men.
Sure, I would ask beside you
No other wealth in life,
But only you and I to be
Together in the glen.

* This translation is in the metre of the original. *Literally*:—
I would wed Courteous Breedyeen, Without coat, shoe, or shirt, Treasure of my heart! If it were possible, for me, I would fast for you nine meals, Without food, without drink, without any share (of anything), On an island in

Ṡeinnfinn ceól ar teudaiḃ
Duit, le bárr mo ṁeura,
Ṫréigfinn mná na h-Éireann ort,
A's leanfainn ṫu 'san tsnáṁ
'S dá mbéiḋinn am' ríġ na Gréige
No am' ṗrionnsa ar na ceudtaiḃ
Do ḃeurfainn suas an méad sin
Do ṗeurla an ḃrollaiġ ḃáin.

Dá bfeicfeá reult an eólais
'S í teaċt i mbeul an ḃóṫair
Déarfá go mbuḋ seód uait
Do ṫógfaḋ ceó a's draoiġeaċt,
A gruaḋ dearg mar rósaiḃ
'S a súil mar drúċt an ḟóġṁair
A béilín tana ró ḋeas
'S a brágaid ar ḋaṫ an aoil.
Ḃí a dá ċíċ corra cóṁ-ċruinn
Ṁol mé í[ad] 's ni mór liom,
'Nn a seasaṁ ag deunaṁ lóċrain
'S iad cearta os cóṁair a croiḋe,
Tá mé i mbrón 's i ndóġraing*
O sgiorr tu uaim tar teórainn,
Ciḋ is fada ó fuair mé cóṁairle
Go ngearrfá-sa ar mo ṡaoġal.

Tosóċad ṡíos i mBréuċ-ḃuiḋe
A's raċfad go Loċ Éirne
O Ṡligeaċ go bonn Céise
Ḃeurfaiḋ mé mo sgríob,
Siúḃalfaiḋ mé Móin-Éile
Corcaiġ a's Beinn-Éidir
'S ni ṡeasfaiḋ me i dTom-gréine
Go dtéiḋ mé go Tráiġliġe.

* "Dorann" 'san MS.

Loch Erne, with desire for me and you to be together Till we should settle our case. O cheek of the colour of the dog-berries, O little cuckoo of the top of the mountain, Do not falsify your promise, But rise up before day, And in spite of the law of the clergy Sure I would choose you for my consort, And, Oh, God, were not that a nice story, A man eloping with his love.

My heart started with trouble, and I frightened nine times, That morning that I heard That you were not to be found, And all the days with merriment I

I'd sing to you and harp you,
I'd know to touch your heart;
And sure I would not part you
For Erin's very best.
And were I King of Greece, or
Any king at peace,
I'd give it all to thee, love,
My pearl of white breast.

O had you seen her moving,
My love who was so cruel!
She was a star-bright jewel
For dispersing fog and mist,
Her cheeks, the rose shone through them,
Her eyes like harvest dew-drops,
Her neck like lime, and truly
Her mouth was to be kissed.
Her breasts so round, two diamonds,
I praised them for their brightness,
Raised up like lamps and shining
Before her burning heart.
And I am, night and morning,
In grievous blight and mourning,
Though often men foretold me
That I should feel their smart.

At Brakewee I'll arise
And walk Loch Erne's islands,
From Kesh I'll search to Sligo
And hunt it all for thee;
And I shall try Monaily,
And Cork and high Ben-Édir,
And stand not in Tomgraney
Until I reach Tralee.

---

and you spent in solitude, Without any one at all guarding us, but the jug and it on the table. If I would find out your tidings The story (*i.e.* case) would go very hard on me (even) if you were to go to the foot of the Reek, or I would cling to my love. And I would sooner be stretched up by you, with nothing under us but heather and rushes, Than be listening to the cuckoos that are stirring at the break of day, *etc.* The literal translation of the fourth verse is as follows:—

If you were to see the star of knowledge And she coming in the mouth of the road, You would say that it was a jewel (at a distance) from you, Who would raise (*i.e.* disperse) fog and enchantment, Her countenance red like the roses, And her eye like the dew of the harvest, Her thin little mouth, very pretty, And her

Níl gleanntán cnoic ná sléiḃe
Ná baile-cuain 'san méad sin
Naċ dtóireóċaiḋ mé má's féidir liom,
'S naċ n-eulóċaiḋ mé le m' ṁian,
Muna ḃfáġ' mé Ḃríġid 'san méad sin
Níl agam le ráḋ léiṫe
Aċt ḃeannaċt slán a's ceud do ċur
le bláṫ na suġ-ċraoḃ.

Tá an oiread eile ann san ḃpíosa so, aċt is cinnte mé naċ leis an ḃfear ceudna é. Tá sé lán suas de ainmneaċaiḃ as na h-úġdaraiḃ Greugaċa agus Rómánaċa, agus is dóiġ gur ag taisbéant a ṁúnaiḋ ⁊ a eólais féin atá an file. Deir se gur casaḋ Mercuri leis agus gur dubairt gur dóiġ gur b'é Pluto do sgiob an cailín leis, agus cuireann an file roiṁe dul go Tartarus le n-a taḃairt amaċ as. Aċt deir sé leis fein ann sin, má ṫéiḋeann sé ann naċ mbéiḋ aon ċongnaṁ mór aige ag troid ar son a ġráḋ-san, óir naċ ḃfuil mórán] cúṁaċta ag na Spánaiġiḃ 'ná ag luċt an Ṗápa ann sin ṡíos, aċt da mbeiḋeaḋ Cranmer Calbin Ḣannraoi no Mártain beó go ḃfuiġfeaḋ sé litir uaṫa ċum a g-cáirdeaḋ ann sin do ḋeunfaḋ an gnó ḋó.

Ní ṁór ḋam * congnaṁ láidir
Ní ḃfuil mé mór mar Charon
D'éidir ḋó mé ḃáṫaḋ
Dá dtigfinn ann a líon,
Tá a ḃád 's a ṁaidiḋe-ráṁa
Go siorruiḋe ann súd ar gáṙda
Ní ṫaitniġeann dream an Pápa leis
Ní ġéilleann sé d'á ndliġe.

Deir sé ann sin go raċfaiḋ se i g-coinne na Féinne Éireann, go dtiucfaiḋ Fionn Goll Osgar Cuċulainn agus Clann Uisneaċ leis agus go mbrisfiḋ se ifrionn le n-a g-congnaṁ-san agus go n-iomċóraiḋ sé a ġráḋ ar ais] arís leis faoi ḃuaiḋ. Is cosṁúil gur fear éigin eile do ċuir na ḃeursaiḋ sin i g-cionn an ṁéid do ṫug mé, agus naċ mbaineann siad ó ċeart leis an g-ceud-ċuid dé.

*=" Ní fuláir ḋam," mar deirid i gCúige Muṁan .i. " is riaċtanaċ dam."

neck of the colour of the lime. Her two breasts were pointed and equal round, I praised them, and thought it not much (to do so) They standing making a lamp And shapen over against her heart, I am in grief and in tribulation Since you slipped from me across the mearing, Though it was long since I was advised That you would shorten my life.

There's never hill nor mountain,
Nor glen nor sheltered fountain,
Nor inch nor harbour's mouth,
But I'll search it all for thee.
And if I cannot find her
My love remains behind her,
I can but blow her blindly
A blessing from me.

There is as much more in this piece, but I am certain that it is not by the same man. It is full up of names taken out of the Greek and Roman authors, and no doubt it is only showing his own learning and knowledge that the poet is. He says that Mercury met him and told him that he was certain that it was Pluto who whipped off the girl with him, and the poet sets before himself to go to Tartarus to take her back out of it. But then he says to himself that if he goes there he will have no great assistance in fighting for his love, for the Spaniards have no great power down there, nor the people of the Pope, but that if Cranmer, Calvin, Henry, or Martin were alive he would get a letter from them to their friends there, which would do the business for him.

I want a strong help;
I am not large like Charon;
He would be able to drown me
If I were to come into his net;
His boat and his oars are
Everlastingly there on guard;
The people of the Pope do not please him,
He does not submit to their law.

He says, then, that he will go for the Fenians of Ireland, until Finn, Goll, Oscar, Cuchulain and the children of Uisneach come with him, and that he will break hell with their help, and carry his love back again with him victoriously. It is likely that it was some other man who added those verses to what I gave before, and that they do not belong by right to the first part of it.

The remainder is easy and need not be translated. *Féirín*, in the third verse means "a present," perhaps from English "fairing." *I ndán dam* means "fated for me." *Ceaptha*, in the fourth verse, means "shapen." *Dorann* is probably written for *Dóghraing*, which means anguish or misery. *Gearr air* = shorten it. *Gearr é* = cut it. I do not know where Moin-Eile, in the fifth verse is. Breuch-bhuidhe, a corruption of Breuch-mhuigh, or Breuch-mhagh "the Wolf's Plain," is a townland in Sligo. Céis is also in Sligo and Tomgréine a little village in Clare.

Caiṫfiḋ mé cúpla abrán beag eile ċur síos ann so, ciḋ naċ cinnte mé ar aon ċor gur Connaċtaiġ do rinne iad. Ni obair daoine-tuaiṫe iad aċt daoine fóġlamṫa. Ag so an ċeud ċeann.

OĊ A ṀUIRE.

Oċ! a Ṁuire naċ truaġ mo ċás
I bpiantaiḃ báis, ar ḃiṫ mo ṡuain,
Fá 'n g-cluanaiġ ṁeangaċ do ṡlad mo ġráḋ
'S naċ ḃfáġaim go bráṫ a malairt uaiṫ'.

Ṁeall sí mise le briaṫraiḃ bláṫ
An ḃéiṫ ġeal* ḃán is gile snuaḋ
Naċ dtréigfeaḋ mé go dti lá an ḃráṫ'
'S anois gur líon sí† lán de m' ḟuaṫ.

Is mairg a ċreidfeas bean go bráṫ
No ḃéarfaḋ i g-cás dí sios a rúin,
Mar do rinne mise do líon d'á gráḋ
'S anois gur náir léiṫe beannuġaḋ dúinn.

Tá an dán so 'nna Rannaiġeaċt Mór fadaiġṫe amaċ; ag so dán eile tá níos coṁúile go mór le fíor-Rannuiġeaċt. Ni ḃfuair mé aon ainm aċt Uilliam Ruaḋ os cionn an abráin seó, aċt is coṁúil gur dán Muiṁneaċ é, óir is focal Muiṁneaċ "puinn" 'san gceud rann;—"morán."

IS AOIBHINN DUIT. Uilliam Ruaḋ cecinit.

Is aoiḃinn duit a ḋuine ḋoill
Naċ ḃfeiceann puinn de na mnáiḃ
Oċ! dá ḃfeicfeá a ḃfeiceann sinn
Do ḃeiḋeá tinn mar atáim.

Is truaġ a Ḋia naċ dall do ḃíos
Sul do ċiḋinn a cúl casta,
A corp sneaċta, slioċt ġeal saor,
Oċ! is saoṫ liom mo ḃeaṫa.

* "An ṁéidġeal," 'san MS.   † "'S gur líon sí anois," 'san MS.

* This translation is in the metre of the original. *Literally* :—
Oh. Mary (*i.e.* Virgin) is it not a pity, my case! In the pains of death in want of my slumber, on account of the guileful deceiver who plundered my love, and I get not for ever an exchange (of her own love) from her. She deceived me with blossoming words, the bright maiden of brightest countenance (saying) that she would not forsake me till the day of judgment, and now she has become full of hatred of me. Alas! for him who shall ever believe in a woman, or shall give in

I must give here a couple more short songs, although I am not at all sure that it was Connacht men who made them. They are not the work of peasants, but of educated people. Here is the first :

UCH ! O MARY.

Oh, Mary, but mine is the pitiful case,
In sorrow's embrace I am left this day,
The little deceiver of roguish face
Has stolen each trace of my heart away.

She swore with words of bewitching grace—
How honest her face did appear alway—
That she would not forsake me through time nor space,
And now she has hastened to shun my way.

Let no man yield to a lovely face,
But his energy brace as best he may ;
She filled me first with her love—'twas base—
Then laughs in my face and turns away.*

This poem is in the great Ranneeught metre lengthened out. Here is another poem a good deal more like true Ranneeught. I found no name but "William Ruadh" to this song, but it is probable that he is a Munster man, for "pween" in the first rann is a Munster word, meaning "a good many."

HAPPY IT IS.*

Happy 'tis, thou blind, for thee
That thou seest not our star ;
Could'st thou see as we now see
Thou would'st be as we now are.

God! why was I not made blind
Ere my mind was set upon her ?
Oh, when I behold her eye,
How can I weigh life or honour ?

---

charge (?) to her a knowledge of his intentions, as I did who was filled with love for her, and now she is loath to (even) salute me.

For this unlawful extension of the Ranneeught metre see the preface. The true Ranneeught has only seven lines in each syllable, while these lines have eight, nine, or ten.

* This is in the metre of the original. *Literally* :—

"It is happy for thee, O blind man, who dost not see much of women. Uch, if you were to see what we see, thou would'st be sick even as I am. It is a pity, O God, that it was not blind I was before I saw her twisted cool. Her snowy body (of) race bright and free, Uch, I think my life a misery. I always thought the blind pitiable until my calamity waxed beyond the grief of all, Then, though it

Daoine dalla buḋ ṫruaġ liom
Gur ḟás mo ġuais tar ṗúḋar ċáiċ,
Ṫugas mo ṫruaġ, cid ṫruaġ, ar ṫnúṫ,
A lúib na lúb ag lúib atáim.

Is mairg riaṁ do ċonnairc í
'S is mairg naċ bḟeiceann í gaċ lá,
Is mairg air a bḟuil snaiḋm d'á searc,
'S is mairg sgaoilte as atá.

Is mairg do ṫéiḋ d'á ḟios
'S is mairg naċ bḟuil d'á ḟios de ġnáṫ,
Is mairg duine bíoḋ 'nna h-aice
'S is mairg naċ 'nna h-aice tá.

Do ṫug mé anois go leór de ṡomplaḋaib ar an abrán-gráḋ mar do cumaḋ é leis na daoinib-tuaiṫe, fir agus mná, agus measaim gur an-beag de na dántaib do ṫug mé ann so do bí déanta le daoinib a raib eólas aca ar ḃárduiġeaċt, no le daoinib do sgríob iad mar ċaṫaḋ-aimsire agus le feuċaint créad d'ḟeudfaḋ siad do ḋéanaṁ ag filiḋeaċt. Aċt, sul sguirim, caiṫfiḋ mé trí no ceaṫar de ḋántaib eile de na sean-dántaib ṫabairt ann so, mar ṡompla ar na h-abránaib gráḋ mar bíodar ameasg na nGaeḋal na ceudta bliaḃain ó ṡoin. Ní ṫig liom a ráḋ cia h-iad na h-úġdair do ċum na dánta so leanas, no cia an t-am do ṁair siad, aċt measaim gur tamall maiṫ ó ṡoin do bí siad, agus is follusaċ go raib siad níos múinte agus níos eólaiġe 'ná na daoine do ċum an méad abrán ṫug mé ċeana. Fuair me iad i láiṁ-sgríbinnib Connaċtaċa agus beirim ann so mar abráin Connaċtaċa iad, aċt leis an ḟírinne d'innsint d'ḟeudfadaois beiṫ cumṫa i n-aon ċúige de na cúigib, óir ni bḟuil difḟir ar biṫ idir an ċanaṁain do bí cleaċtaiġṫe leis na bárdaib dá ċeud bliaḋain no trí ceud bliaḋain ó ṡoin i n-aon ċúige de na cúigib. Do ḃainfidís na h-abráin leanas, ó ċeart, do ċruinniuġaḋ na briosa sin d'ḟág na fíor-ḃáird 'nna

is a pity, my pity I turned into envy, In a loop of the loops in a loop am I. It is woe for whoever saw her. And it is woe for him who sees her not each day. It is woe for him on whom the knot of her love is (tied), And it is woe for him who is loosed out of it. It is woe for him who goes to her, and it is woe for him who is not with her constantly. It is woe for a person to be near her, And it is a woe for him that is not near her.

There is a sixth verse which I do not give above as I do not understand it. It runs thus—

A hainm bhios ag sgolta srotha
San ruadh mhuir ó sloingtear ise,
O na searc ní'l saor acht dalla
Ger b'faith aitis liom a feicsin.

Once I pitied sightless men,
  I was then unhurt by sight,
Now I envy those who see not,
  They can be not hurt by light.

Woe who once has seen her please,
  And then sees her not each hour,
Woe for him her love-mesh traps,
  Woe for whom it snaps its power.

Woe for him who visits not,
  Woe his lot who does, I wis,
Woe for him is not beside her,
  Woe besides for him who is.

I have now given enough of examples of the love song as it was composed by the peasantry, both men and women, and I think that it is very few of the love songs given here which were composed by people who had a knowledge of bardism, or by people who wrote them for pastime, and only to try what they could do in the way of poetry. But before I leave off I must give three or four more poems, of the older ones, for examples of the love songs as they were amongst the Gael some hundreds of years ago. I cannot say who are the authors who composed the following poems, or what was the time at which they lived, but I think it was a good while ago that they existed, and it is evident that they were more learned and more educated than the people who wrote the songs I have given already. I found them in Connacht MSS., and give them here as Connacht songs, but to tell the truth, they might be composed in any of the provinces, for there is no difference at all between the dialects used by the bards two or three hundred years ago in any of the five provinces. The songs which follow would by right belong to a

---

This verse appears to contain a cryptic allusion to the girl's name, a thing which is not unusual with the older poets. My friend Tomás O Flannaoile has suggested to me that the girl's name was probably "Muireann Ruadh," for the translation of the first line appears to be this, "Her name is (found) by dividing the waters in the Red Sea, whence she is called." Hence it is a pun upon *muir* "sea," and *rann* or *roinn*, "a division." The last two ranns seem to be a Gaelic extension of the Latin pentameter,

"*Non possum tecum vivere nec sine te.*"

The meaning of the last line of the third verse is not very clear; it seems to contain a kind of pun or paronomasia on *lúb*, a "curl" and *lúb* a "noose." I do not well understand the force of the preposition "ag," in *ag lúb*. The phrase seems to mean "snared." Perhaps a better translation would be "*in the snare of all snares* (*i.e.* woman's love) *ensnared am I.*" Literally, *a snare has me*."

Although the word *puinn* is often used in Munster for "many," it seems to be here used [in the sense of "jot" or "tittle," and is probably borrowed from the

ndiaiġ, agus ní d'abránaib na ndaoine-tuaiṫe atá mé ag tabairt ann san leabar so. Aċt is cosṁúil naċ bfuil na píosaiḋ seo ró ṡean, ciḋ go bfuil siad i miosúr riaġalta, no má tá siad sean, féin, d'aṫruiġeaḋ iad rud beag ó cumaḋ iad, leis na daoinib do ġab agus do sgríob iad, óir ní'l mórán focal i n-aon ċeann aca naċ bfuil ċoṁ soilléir so-ṫuigṫe anois agus bí siad ariaṁ. Agus sin é an t-áḋbar beirim ann so iad, óir is dóiġ liom gur cuiṁnuiġeaḋ leis na daoinib iad, agus gur sgríobaḋ síos go déiġeannaċ iad, óir ní bfuair me aċt ceann aca i n-aon sean-sgríbinn. Agus mar is i sgríbinnib Connaċtaċa fuair mé iad ní mi-ċeart ar fad é, ait do ṫabairt dóib ameasg na n-abrán gráḋ so.

Breaṫnóċaiḋ an léiġṫeóir leis an g-ceud aṁarc an diṫfir an-ṁór atá idir na h-oibreaċaib seo na mbárd fóġlaṁṫa smuáinteaċ, agus na ndaoine tíre. Ag so an ċeud ċeann beursfas mé.

AN SEARC 'GÁ ḊIÚLTUĠAḊ.

Mo ġráḋ, ón 'sí mo ġráḋ
An bean is mó bíos 'g am' ċráḋ,
Is annsa í ó m' ḋéanaṁ tinn
Ná an bean do m' ḋéanaṁ slán.

'Sí mo stór, ón 'sí mo stór,
Bean an roisg uaiṫne mar an rós,
Bean naċ g-cuirfeaḋ láṁ fá m' ċeann
Bean naċ luiḋfeaḋ liom ar ór.

Sí mo ṡearc, ón 'sí mo ṡearc
An bean nár ḟág ionnam neart,
Bean naċ leigfeaḋ mo ḋiaiġ oċ
Bean naċ g-cuirfeaḋ liag am' leaċt.

'Sí mo rún, ón 'sí mo rún
Bean naċ n-innseann aon níḋ ḋúinn,
Bean naċ leigfeaḋ am' ḋiaiġ oċ,
Bean naċ ndeunfaḋ sile súl.

Norman *point*, in imitation of the French idiom, *qui ne voit point de femme*, to which it is here exactly equivalent.

An attempt is made to retain for the first verse of the translation the inwoven vowel rhyme of the original.

Coulds't THOU SEE as WE NOW SEE
THOU *would'st* BE as WE NOW are.

* This translation is in the metre of the original, only more regular. *Literally.* My love, oh ! she is my love, The woman who is most for destroying me ; Dearer is she from making me ill Than the woman who would be for making me well. She is my treasure, Oh, she is my treasure, The woman of the grey

collection of those pieces which the true bards left after them, and not to the songs of the peasantry which I am giving in this collection. But it is likely that these pieces are not very old, though they are in a regular metre, or, if they are old, itself, they were somewhat changed since they were composed, by the people who sang them and wrote them down, for there are not many words in any of them which are not as clear and intelligible now as they ever were. And for this reason I give them here, for I am sure they were remembered by the people and lately written down by them, for I have not found any of them except one, the "Roman Earl," in an old manuscript. And as it was in Connacht manuscripts I found them, it is not altogether wrong to give a place to them here amongst these love songs. The reader will observe at the first glance the very great difference that there is between these works of the educated, thinking bards, and those of the country people. This is the first one I shall give :

MY LOVE, OH, SHE IS MY LOVE.*

She casts a spell, oh, casts a spell,
Which haunts me more than I can tell.
Dearer, because she makes me ill,
Than who would will to make me well.

She is my store, oh, she my store,
Whose grey eye wounded me so sore,
Who will not place in mine her palm,
Who will not calm me any more.

She is my pet, oh, she my pet,
Whom I can never more forget ;
Who would not lose by me one moan,
Nor stone upon my cairn set.

She is my roon, oh, she my roon,
Who tells me nothing, leaves me soon ;
Who would not lose by me one sigh,
Were death and I within one room.

(?) eye (she) like the rose, A woman who would not place a hand beneath my head, A woman who would not be with me for gold. She is my affection, Oh ! she is my affection, The woman who left no strength in me ; A woman who would not breathe a sigh after me, A woman who would not raise a stone at my tomb. She is my secret love, Oh ! she is my secret love, A woman who tells us (*i. e.*, me) nothing ; A woman who would not breathe a sigh after me, A woman who would not (for me) shed tears.* She is my shape, Oh ! she is my shape,† A woman who does not remember me to be out, A woman who would not

'Sí mo ċruṫ, ón 'sí mo ċruṫ,
Bean naċ g-cuiṁnuiġeann mé beiṫ amuiġ,
Bean naċ ngoilfeaḋ uair mo ḃáis*
'Sí ċráḋaiġ mo ċroiḋe go lár.†

Mór mo ċás, ón mór mo ċás
Is iongnaḋ ḟad go ḃfáġaim bás,
Bean naċ dtiúḃraḋ taoḃ liom
Dar mo ṁionn is í mo ġráḋ.

'S í mo roġan, ón 'sí mo roġan
Bean naċ ndearcfaḋ siar orm,
An ḃean naċ ndeunfaḋ liom-sa síṫ
(A's) tá de ṡíor lán de ġráin.

Is mór mo ḃrón, ón 's mór mo ḃrón
Fá an droċ-ṁeas mór
Ag an mnaoi do mo ċlaoiḋ'
Is í ṡlad mé ó mo ḃeó.

'S í mo ṁian, ón 'sí mo ṁian,
Bean is annsa liom faoi 'n ngréin,
An ḃean naċ g-cuirfeaḋ orm binn
Dá suiḋfinn le na taéḃ.

'Sí do ċráḋaiġ mo ċroiḋe
A's d'ḟágbuiġ osna am' lár,‡
Muna dtóġṫar an t-olc so óm' ċroiḋe
Ní ḃéiḋ mé go deó slán.

* "uiri mo ḃás" 'san MS. † "gan larr" 'san MS.
‡ "ionnam ċoiḋċ" 'san MS.

cry at the hour of my death, It is she ruined my heart to its middle. Great my case, Oh! great my case, It is a wonder how long it is till I find death. A woman who would not give me trust, By my oath she is my love! She is my choice, Oh! she is my choice, The woman who would not look back at me, The woman who would not make peace with me. And who is ever full of hate. Great my grief, Oh! great my grief, At the great disrespect The woman has (working) for my destroying. 'Tis she spoiled me of my life. She is my desire, Oh! she is my desire; A woman dearest to me under the sun, The woman who would not pay me heed, If I were to sit by her side. It is she ruined my heart, And left a sigh for ever in me. Unless this evil be raised off my heart, I shall not be well for ever.

She is my dear, oh, she my dear,
Who cares not whether I be here.
Who would not weep when I am dead,
Who makes me shed the silent tear.

Hard my case, oh, hard my case,
How have I lived so long a space,
She does not trust me any more,
But I adore her silent face.

She is my choice, oh, she my choice,
Who never made me to rejoice;
Who caused my heart to ache so oft,
Who put no softness in her voice.

Great my grief, oh, great my grief,
Neglected, scorned beyond belief,
By her who looks at me askance,
By her who grants me no relief.

She's my desire, oh, my desire,
More glorious than the bright sun's fire;
Who were than wind-blown ice more cold,
Had I the boldness to sit by her.

She it is who stole my heart,
But left a void and aching smart,
And if she soften not her eye
Then life and I shall shortly part.

---

* *Literally, "Who would not make a pouring of eyes."*

† *Perhaps* cruṫ *is for* croṫ = *riches or cattle. But an old meaning of* cruṫ *is destruction, which would make best sense if it were not too obsolete. He may have meant to say "she is my riches." The word generally means "shape" which seems to make no sense here, unless, perhaps, like the Latin "forma" and "formosus," it is used in the sense of "beauty." Compare* a chrothach mar cholum *in the old Litany of Mary in the Leabhar Breac = formosa ut Columba, beautiful as a dove.*

Is iomḋa earráid agus tuisleaḋ i miosúr na línteaḋ seó, agus is comarṫa é sin naċ ḃfuil siad againn ann so mar ṫáinig siad o láiṁ an ḟile. Ag so an dara giota.

Ni ḃfág mise bás duit.

Ni ḃfáġ mise bás duit
A ḃean úd an ċuirp mar ġéis,
Daoine leaṁa do ṁarḃais riaṁ
Ni ionnann iad a's mé féin.

Créad fáṫ raċfainn d'eug
Do'n ġob dearg, do'n deud mar ḃláṫ (?)
An cruṫ ṁíonla, an t-uċt mar ġéis,
An dóiḃ súd ġeaḃainn féin bás?

Na cíoċa corra, an cneas úr,
Na gruaḋa corcra, an cúl siar,
Go deiṁin ni ḃfuiġfead-sa bás
Dóiḃ súd, go mbuḋ áill le Dia.

Do ṁalaiḋ * caola, d'ḟolt mar ór,
Do rún geanmaiḋe, do ġlór leisg,
Do ḟál ċruinn, do ċolpa réiḋ,
Ni ṁarḃfaid siad aċt duine leaṁ.

Do ṁéin aoiḃ, d'aigne saor,
Do ḃos tana, do ṫaoḃ mar ċuip,
Do rosg gorm, do ḃráġad bán,
Ni ḃfáġ mise bás duit.

A ḃean úd, an ċuirp mar ġéis,
Do h-oileaḋ mé ag duine glic,
A ḃos ṫana, a ḃráiġe ḃáin
Ní ḃfág mise bás duit.

Ag so anois an tríoṁaḋ giota. Ní'l sé ċoṁ sean leis an dá ċeann ṫuas, creidim. Ní'l an file ċoṁ fuair-ġlic leis an mbárd déiġeannaċ, agus ni ċroideann sé anaġaiḋ an ġráḋ atá 'gá ċiapaḋ.

* "mailiġe" 'san MS.

This translation is exactly in the metre of the original, *Literally.*
I shall not die for thee, O woman yonder, of body like a swan. Silly people (were they) thou hast ever slain. They and myself are not the same. Why should I go to die For the red lip, for the teeth like blossoms; The gentle

There is many a mistake and error in the metre of these lines, in the Irish, and that is a proof that we have not got them here just as they came from the hands of the poet. Here is the second piece :—

I SHALL NOT DIE FOR THEE.

For thee I shall not die,
Woman high of fame and name ;
Foolish men thou mayest slay
I and they are not the same.

Why should I expire
For the fire of any eye,
Slender waist or swan-like limb,
Is't for them that I should die ?

The round breasts, the fresh skin,
Cheeks crimson, hair so long and rich ;
Indeed, indeed, I shall not die,
Please God, not I, for any such.

The golden hair, the forehead thin,
The chaste mien, the gracious ease,
The rounded heel, the languid tone,
Fools alone find death from these.

Thy sharp wit, thy perfect calm,
Thy thin palm like foam of sea ;
Thy white neck, thy blue eye,
I shall not die for thee.

Woman, graceful as the swan,
A wise man did nurture me,
Little palm, white neck, bright eye,
I shall not die for ye.

Here now is the third piece. It is not as old, I think, as the two given above. The poet is not so coldly-wise as the last bard, and does not fight against the love that is torturing him.

---

figure, the breast like a swan, Is it for them I myself should die. The pointed (?) breasts, the fresh skin ; The scarlet cheeks, the undulating cool ; Indeed, then, I shall not die For them, may it please God. Thy narrow brows, thy tresses like gold, Thy chaste secret, thy languid voice, Thy heel round, thy calf smooth. They shall slay none but a silly person. Thy delightful mien, thy free spirit, Thy thin palm, thy side like foam, Thy blue eye, thy white throat!—I shall not die for thee. O woman of body like a swan, I was nurtured by a cunning man, O thin palm, O white bosom—I shall not die for thee.

An Naoiḋ Beag Ṡiar.

Goirim ṫu, a naoiḋ ḃig ṡiar
Na ḃfolt fiar, ar ḋaṫ an óir,
'S gaċ dual díoḃ go fada fann
Naċ gann do ṡín go bárr an ḟeóir.

Na rosg liaṫ, na ḃreucain mall,
Na malaiḋ* ngann mar sgríb pinn,
Na ngruaḋ mbán aċt corcair tríoṫa
Oċón ! is tríoṫa táim tinn.

An beul blasta, ar ṡnuaḋ caoin,
'S an deud ċailce,† ṡaor ar ṁéid,
An tsrón ḋeas, an smig naċ mór,
'S an ṗíoḃ ḃán, snuaḋ de'n ngéis.

Na méur n-úr, na ngeal-láṁ nglan,
Na ngeug lag dá n-iaḋann (?) ciúin
Do gaċ ceól síġ-ḃinn saor-ḃláiṫ
Do sgríoḃ an ḟaoileann ḃán dúinn ‡

An t-uċt mar aol na g-cíoċ g-cruinn
Ariaṁ fós nár ḋórn aon, §
An corp séiṁ seang, an taoḃ ḃláiṫ,
Ní ṡeinnim daoiḃ dáil mo ġéis'.

Is truaġ gan mé astiġ faoi ġlas
Ag mnaoi na mbas méar-glac-maoiṫ,
I Portláirge na slios nglan
No i liosgaṁail na sreaḃ g-caoin.

Ag so faoi ḋeireaḋ, cóṁairle—is dóiġ le sean duine gruama éigin—anaġaiḋ na mban, aon ṗíosa beag aṁáin le caṫaḋ, mar ṁeaḃċan suaraċ, ann san taoiḃ eile de'n sgéala, andiaiġ an ṁéid sin molta. Is fiú a ṫabairt mar ġeall ar an iarraċt do rinne an bárd sgeul d'innsint. Is sompla maiṫ ar ṁóḋ na sean-ḃárd

* "mailiġe" 'san MS. † "Ċailce ḃán" 'san MS.

‡ "ḟionn" 'san MS. agus labairṫear é i n-áiteaċaiḃ i gCúige Múṁan mar "fiúnn" aċt i gConnaċtaiḃ mar "finn." Ní focal coitċionn ameasg na g-Connaċtaċ anois é. § "fear" 'san MS.

LITTLE CHILD, I CALL THEE.

Little child, I call thee fair,
Clad in hair of golden hue,
Every lock in ringlets falling
Down, to almost kiss the dew.

Slow grey eye and languid mien,
Brows as thin as stroke of quill,
Cheeks of white with scarlet through them,
Och! it's through them I am ill.

Luscious mouth, delicious breath,
Chalk-white teeth, and very small,
Lovely nose and little chin,
White neck, thin, she is swan-like all.

Pure white hand and shapely finger,
Limbs that linger like a song;
Music speaks in every motion
Of my sea-mew warm and young.

Rounded breasts and lime-white bosom,
Like a blossom, touched of none,
Stately form and slender waist,
Far more graceful than the swan.

Alas for me! I would I were
With her of the soft-fingered palm,
In Waterford to steal a kiss,
Or by the Liss whose airs are balm.

---

* This translation is in the exact metre of the original. *Literally*:—
I call on thee, O little baby over there,* Of the undulating tresses of the colour of gold; And every lock of them long and languid, That almost stretch to the top of the grass; Of the grey eyes of the slow looks, Of the brows thin like the stroke of a pen, Of the white cheeks, but scarlet through them, Ochone, it is through them I am ill. The tasteful mouth of the hue of a berry, And the chalk-white teeth free from size (?) The pretty nose, the chin not large, And the white throat, appearance of the swan. Of the fresh fingers of white hands clean (cut), Of the languid limbs round which close tunes (?) Of every fairy-sweet free-blossomed music Which (she) the white fair seagull wrote. The bosom like lime, of the rounded breasts, That never yet any touched; The gentle tender body, the blossom-like side—I sing ye not (half) an account of my swan. 'Tis pity I am not in under lock With the woman of the palms of the soft-finger touch, In Portlarigy (Waterford) of the clean benches (?) Or in Lisgowal of the gentle streams.
* *Literally, "little infant, west."*

é, agus tá an píosa so coitċionn go leór, ṫarraing mise é as sgríbinn atá agam do rinne Doċtúir O Donabáin an Sgoláire mór Gaeḋeilge. D'aṫraiġ mise litriuġaḋ na bfocal.

AN T-IARLA BHI 'SAN RÓIṀ.

Mairg do ġníḋ cumann leis na mnáiḃ
  Ní mar sin atáid na fir,
  Do buḋ ċóir a g-cur i g-cré
  I n-éagmais na mban so astiġ.

Iarla glic do bí 'san Róiṁ
  Ag a mbiḋeaḋ coirn óir fá ḟíon,
  Ar ṁnaoi an Iarla ṁóir ṁaiṫ
  Do ċualaḋ sgeul ait, má b'ḟíor.

Lá d'á rabadar araon
  Taob le taob ar leabaiḋ clúiṁ
  Do leig [sé] air go raiḃ ag éag
  Do ċum sgeul, do ḃraiṫ a rúin.

"Oċ! oċ! dá bfuiġeá-sa bás
  Buḋ beag mo ċás ionnam féin,
  Ar boċtaiḃ Dé leaṫ ar leaṫ
  Do roinfinn fá seaċ mo spré.

Do ċuirfinn síoda agus sról
  I g-coṁ-roinn fairsing d'ór dearg
  I dtimċioll do ċuirp 'san uaiġ,"
  Ars an bean do smuain* an ċealg.

Deónaiġtear leisean an bás
  Do ḃraiṫ mná no mala seang,
  D'á deóin níor ċúṁaill sí sin
  An ḃeóiḋ a fir, niḋ d'ar' ġeall.

---

* Labairtear an focal so mar "smaoin" anois, ann gaċ áit i n-Éirinn creidim, aċt is follasaċ ó'n rann so gur labaireaḋ é an t-am sin "smuain" mar sgríoḃtar é, ag deunaṁ coṁ-fuaime le uaiġ.

This translation is in the metre of the original. *Literally.*

Pity of him who enters on affection with women, Not so are the men. They ought to be put in clay, Without (the co-operation) of these women inside. A wise Earl there was in Rome, Who used to have golden goblets under wine, About the wife of the great good Earl There was heard a pleasant (*or* queer) story, if true.

Here, at last, is a counsel against women, given by some morose old man, no doubt; only one little piece to throw in as a petty make-weight on the other side of the balance, after all that praise. It is worth giving on account of the attempt the bard has made to tell a story. It is a good example of the manner of the old bards, and this piece is common enough. I took it out of a manuscript which I have, made by Doctor O'Donovan, the greatest of Irish scholars. I have somewhat changed the orthography:

THE ROMAN EARL.

No man's trust let woman claim,
Not the same as men are they;
Let the wife withdraw her face
When ye place the man in clay.

Once there was in Rome an earl
Cups of pearl did hold his ale,
Of this wealthiest earl's mate
Men relate a famous tale.

So it chanced that of a day
As they lay at ease reclined,
He in jest pretends to die,
Thus to try her secret mind.

"Och! Ochone, if you should die,
Never I would be myself;
To the poor of God I'd give
All my living, lands and pelf.

"Then in satin stiff with gold,
I would fold thy fair limbs still,
Laying thee in gorgeous tomb,"
Said the woman bent on ill.

Soon the earl, as if in death,
Yielded up his breath to try her;
Not one promise kept his spouse
Of the vows made glibly by her.

On a day that they were together, Side by side on a bed of down, He let on that he was dying. He shaped a story to spy out her secret mind. "Och! Och! if thou wert to die Little would be my regard for my own life (*literally*, small were my case in myself). On the poor of God, round about, I would divide severally my fortune. I would put silk and satin, In an equal-broad division of red gold, Round about thy body in the tomb,"—

Fuair d'á ṁalairt ar an sráid
An tráṫ sin—cid 'r beag an stór,
Dá bann-láiṁ no trí de ṡac
Naċ ráinig ar fad a ṫóin.

Do ġeal sise bréid a cinn
Ar ndul do'n ċill leis an g-corp,
Ni ṫug pigin d' eaglais Dé
'S ni ṫug déirc do ḋuine boċt.

Tugaḋ leisean éirige prap
Nuair bí a bean ag dul uaiḋ,
D'ḟiafraiġ créad fá raiḃ a ċorp
D'á ċur noċt ann san uaiġ.

Ṫug sise leiṫsgeul gar,
Ar nós na mban bíos le h-olc,
D'á saoraḋ ar a fear féin,
Bean naċ ngeoḃaḋ géill i loċt.*

"Braiṫlín fá ċosaiḃ gaċ fir
Ni béiḋ anois mar do bí riaṁ,
Go roisir † go Riġ na ndúil,
Buḋ leat tús ó a dtéid 'san tsliaḃ.

Do ċoiṁ-ling le tús na sluaiġ
Ar ṡliaḃ Sionn—cruaiḋ an cás,
Do ċumas duit aisléine gearr
Naċ ráinig meall do ḋá ṁás."

As na mnáiḃ cid mór bur ndóiġ
Fada dóiḃ ag dul le gaoiṫ,
Tearc duine naċ meallaid siad,
Mairg leigeas a rún le mnaoi.

* "Bean nár gabaḋ geill a loċt" 'san MS. † Go roisir=go riġiḋ tu, go dtig tu go.

Said the woman who thought the deceit. Death is pretended † by him, To spy the woman of the slender brow, Of her will she did not fulfil—After her husband—one thing of all she promised. He got in exchange of it on the street, That time—though it was small its worth—Two cubits or three of sackcloth That did not completely reach even his hips. She brightened the kerchief of her head On

Jerked into a coffin hard,
    With a yard of canvas coarse;
(To his hips it did not come);
    To the tomb they drove the corse.

Bravely dressed was she that day,
    On her way to Mass and grave;
To God's Church and needy men,
    Not one penny piece she gave.

Up he starts, the coffined man,
    Calls upon his wife aloud,
"Why am I thus thrust away,
    Almost naked, with no shroud?"

Then as women do when caught
    In a fault, with ready wit
Answered she upon the wing—
    Not one thing would she admit:

"Winding-sheets are out of date,
    All men state it. Clad like this,
When the judgment trump shall sound,
    You shall bound to God and bliss.

"When in shrouds they trip and stumble
    You'll be nimble then as erst,
Hence I shaped thee this short vest,
    You'll run best and come in first."

Trust not to a woman's faith,
    'Tis a breath, a broken stem;
Few whom they do not deceive,
    Let him grieve that trusts to them.

---

going to the grave-yard with the body, She gave not a penny to the Church of God, And she gave no alms to any poor person. A quick leap up was given by him, When his wife was going away from him. He asked her why his body was A-burying naked in the grave. She gave a ready excuse, After the manner of women (caught) in evil, Clearing herself to her own husband. A woman who would not make submission (?) in fault. "A (winding) sheet round the feet of every man, There shall not be now, as ever before, That thou mayest reach to the king of the elements, Thou shalt have the first place of all that go on the mountain.* To (let thee) race in the front of the multitudes, On the mountain of Sion—

Ciḋ 'r b'iomḋa canafás mín
Agus braiṫlín caol ann a tiġ,
Niḋ le a ḃfolóċaiḋe a noċt
Níor ċuir sí fá ċorp a fir.

Ag sin cumann na mná,
[Ar] san Iarla glic buḋ ġlan gnaoi,
"Féaċaḋ gaċ neaċ clár dó féin
Sul ḟágfas a spré ag a ṁnaoi."

Ag fáġail báis dá mbeiḋeaḋ fear
Ná cluineaḋ a bean é os árd,
D'á ḋeóin na leigeaḋ amaċ
Oċ ná aċ, ciḋ mór a ṁairg.

Tá mé réiḋ anois leis na h-abránaib gráḋ. Ní ṫiúbraiḋ mé aon ċeann eile ann so. Ní'l aon ċineál abrán ameasg na ndaoine-tuaiṫe is iomadaṁla ná iad so. An deiċ-fiċead no dá-fiċead aca do ṫug mé ann so, do ṫóg mé amaċ iad ameasg na g-ceudta, rud naċ raib ro ḟoras le deunaṁ, óir atá an ċuid is mó aca ċoṁ truaillıġṫe agus ċoṁ measgta tríd a ċéile gur deacair é aon ordugaḋ ceart do ċur orra. An méad do ṫug me go dti seó, déanadaois mar ṡomplaḋaib ar an g-caoi ann a g-cuireann an tuataċ Connaċtaċ a smuainte grád i n-abránaib agus i ranntaib, má's dóċċas no eudóċċas, má's brón no lúṫġáire bíos 'gá cor-ruġaḋ.

---

hard the case—I shaped for thee a short shroud That did not reach thy two hips." In women though great is your confidence, It is long known that they go with the wind. Few are the people they do not deceive. Woe is he who lets his secret with a woman. Though many was the piece of smooth canvas, And narrow sheet in her house, A thing by which his nakedness would be covered, She did not put round the body of her husband. There is the affection of the woman! Says the prudent earl of clear countenance—" Let each man look for a coffin for himself, Before he leaves his fortune to his wife." At point of death though a man should be, Let not his wife hear him (sigh) aloud, If he can help it let him not let out, Either Och or Ach, though great be his woe.

Though full her house of linen web,
And sheets of thread spun full and fair
(A warning let it be to us)
She left her husband naked there.

Spake the prudent earl—"In sooth
Woman's truth ye here behold;
Now let each his coffin buy,
Ere his wife shall get his gold.

"When death wrestles for his life
Let his wife not hear him moan;
Great though be his pain and fear,
Let her hear not sigh nor groan."

I have now done with the love songs. I shall give no other of them here. There is no sort of song amongst the peasantry more plentiful than they. The thirty or forty of them which I have given here, I chose out from amongst hundreds, a thing that was not very easy to do, for the most of them are so corrupt and so mixed through each other that it is difficult to get them into any right order. All that I have given up to this let them serve as examples of the way in which the Connacht peasant puts his love-thoughts into song and verse, whether it be hope or despair, grief or joy, that affect him.

† Deónaiġ *means to grant or consent, but here it must mean pretend, or something equivalent.*

‡ *The "Day of the Mountain" is a common phrase for "Judgment Day." She means that not being entangled in a winding-sheet he shall have first place in the running on that day.*

§ *Literally, "long for them going with wind."*

‖ *Literally, "of his will."*

NOTES.

Page 2, line 2. The reader will observe throughout the first half of this book some confusion between ar and air. This must be attributed to the way in which these songs made their appearance. On the death of the *Nation* the *Weekly Freeman* patriotically seconded my efforts to preserve and popularise these songs by placing every two or three weeks a column or two at my disposal. Consequently the publication of these pieces, few as they are, necessarily extended over a long period, during which I changed my views upon the orthography of air, and insensibly fell into the way of writing, with Keating and our older authors, the simple preposition "ar," "on," reserving the spelling air for the compound preposition "on him." In speaking, however, I may observe that both are pronounced in the same way, like *errh*, or like the first syllable in the English word "error." Line 14, for spórṫaṁla, *read* spórtaṁla.

Page 4, line 14, for as *read* is. Line 22, ná is here confounded with no. In Connacht the best speakers and writers use ná after a negative and no on other occasions, as dá mbeiḋeaḋ bean no clann agam, but ní'l ḃean ná clann agam. In Ulster no seems to be often used in both cases. Mr. O'Faherty, in his capital book, "Siamsa an ġeiṁriḋ," has printed the second verse of this song at p. 50, as belonging to a poem which he entitles cóṁairle, one of the sweetest in the whole book. This is the only verse in it which bears any resemblance to mine.

Page 8. The beautiful third verse of this song has found its way into different pieces recited by the people, as into the song "Dá mbeiḋ' spré ag an g-cat" not given here, and others, so that it is hard now to tell to which it properly belongs.

Page 12, line 23 for cóir *read* ċóir.

Page 14, line 1. Ḟé is a dialectic form of fá, the Connacht faoi, which is also sometimes found as fo. In the last line but one, *read* sgríoḃṫa for sgroḃṫa.

Page 16, line 12. i g-clúid a ċéile has been mistranslated in the text as though it were le ċéile. The real translation is, "in one another's protection (or society)." Line 18, mo ḋlaoiġ mar áirne, *i.e.* my sloe-black hair. Line 21, siolla means a "whiff" of wind here; in the tale of *Osgar na Súiste*, which I printed in the *Revue Celtique*, it

means a "glint" of a sunbeam, hence it seems to be applied to anything short or small. Its usual meaning, however, is "syllable," as in the song of Una Péucaċ, at p. 122, but it seems doubtful whether it is derived from the Latin *syllaba* or not. If it is, the use of the English word "jot," and, possibly, the Irish giota, to signify something small, from the Greek *iota*, is a close parallel. Line 32. By right the d of dualaiġ should be aspirated, but aspiration in the case of d and t is not always rigorously observed. Cf Bean Dub an Ġleanna *not* Bean ḋub, etc.

Page 18, line 7, for ḋá *read* dá. Line 9, this line is mistranslated in the text as a correspondent has pointed out to me. It should be "like snow a-winnowing on mountains." This word caiṫ has in modern Connacht usage a great many meanings, as "throw," "winnow," "smoke (tobacco)," "eat," "shoot," "wear (rings, etc.)," "spend (money)," "wear out (clothes, etc.):" in fact, it is a good Gaelic rival to Mark Twain's *Zug*, of which that humorist observes that the thing which this Teutonic monosyllable does *not* mean, when all its legitimate pendants are hung on, has not yet been discovered. By the way, when the verbal participle has a passive sense, as here, it is better to write d'á before it, not 'gá, which should be used, as Dr. Atkinson has shown, only when the participle has an active meaning; then tá sé 'gá (*i.e.* ag a) ḃualaḋ, 'gá ċaṫaḋ, etc., means "he is a-beating it, a-winnowing it," etc., but tá sé d'á (*i.e.* do a) ḃualaḋ, d'á ċaṫaḋ, etc. means, "it is a-beating, a-winnowing," *i.e.*, is being beaten, being winnowed.

Page 20, line 21. This line should be translated "not long was my lying." It is translated as if níor ḃfada was mór fada. Line 25. I think this fánaċ should be translated "sorrowfully."

Page 22, line 30. Slán beó leat is wrongly translated in the text. It means "may you be well while alive," or, "farewell as long as you live."

Page 24. My friend, Seaġán O Ruaiḋriġ (John Rogers), a Mayo man himself, and an authority on Mayo songs, says that the first two verses of this song, Is fada mé ag imṫeaċt, belong by right to the song at p. 34, the right name of which is Máire an ċúil báin, and that this Maurya was an O'Neill who lived at the foot of Knocknashee, (cnoc na síḋe) below Tubbercurry, in the County Sligo. The man who made the song is said to have actually left the country, taking Maurya with him. He also thinks that the third and last two verses of this song are an addition to *Máire an chúil bháin.* The re-

maining four verses are to the measure and air of "Péarla deas an tsléibh báin." The fourth verse of the song at p. 70 of Siamsa an Geimhridh is nearly identical with the first verse of mine, but that song appears to be made up of verses from four different ones.

Page 28, line 19. Cossuaidh is generally Anglicized "Morrisroe." I do not know why she was called Crummey in English.

Page 30. Some say that this most celebrated song had its origin near Buninadden, in Sligo. Seághan O Ruaidhrigh thinks it came from Ballinlough, in West Roscommon. The third line often runs sneachta síobadh 's é d'á séideadh thar shliabh Ui Fhloinn. When the snow is driven low and hard, it is said to a' síobadh or sweeping.

Page 32, line 17, for dílis (the vocative masculine) *read* dílеas (the voc. fem.) There is, however, no appreciable difference in pronunciation. Line 5, aspirate the s of seasc. Line 6, léigeasfadaois is pronounced either *lice-a-deesh* or *lace-a-deesh*, indifferently. The surname Green mentioned in the last line is, I believe, properly O h-Uaithne, and should be anglicized O'Hooney.

Page 34, three lines from bottom, Líne ought to be feminine, not masculine, as here.

Page 36. The last verse of the song called the Ciomach at p. 41, of Mr. O'Faherty's excellent "Siamsa an Geimhridh" is very like the opening verse of my Táilliúirín, but there is no other resemblance between the two pieces. He afterwards recovered a verse nearly identical with my second verse, and prints it on the last page of his book as belonging to the Ciomach. If this is so, my song is a fragment of it, but I think it more likely that they are different pieces altogether, for I have recovered from a Roscommon man another version of his called the Giobach, which I do not give here. Both ciomach and giobach mean the "untidy" or "slatternly" person.

Page 38, line 4. *Read* sé sin for sésin. Line 10. Read di-se for dí-se, for when pronouns are emphasized by a suffix the tendency is for the long vowel to become short, as mise (mish-a) from mé; eisean (esh-in) from é, tusa (thussa or thissa) from tú, etc. Line 25 would be better translated "with desire to marry you."

Page 40, line 29. This beautiful song is also printed by Mr. O'Faherty at p. 42 of the Siamsa. According to him it was generally sung in Connemara as an addition to the song of the "Ciomach," but it is evidently, as he has observed, a completely different piece.

Page 42, line 18, this callaidhe is, I take it, the syllable "caul" of the word High-caul cap, or High-cauled cap (a species of headdress

once much worn) Gaelicized. The term High-caul cap itself, occurs in the song of Youghal Harbour, or, Dul go h-Eoċaill, a most popular one in Connacht, and there is a celebrated air of the same name. This headdress was in vogue during the latter end of the last century and the beginning of this, but I have been unable to discover the origin of the name. The bards disliked the cap, and, as in the case of that contemporaneous article of female attire, the Cardinel, they satirized severely those who wore it.

Page 48, line 19, for bud *read* buḋ. Line 38, for fásġaḋ *read* fásgaḋ.

Page 50, line 4, for lies *read* leis.

Page 56, line 6. Seáġan O Ruaiḋriġ has since explained this word to me. He says it is the Mayo "vernacular for answer in reply to a call or shout, as distinct from an answer to a question, which is freagra, or, as we called it, freagairt." "I remember," he adds, "the episode of the ford of the river, but I never could learn where it was, and did not hear the name Donogue till seeing it in your song." I got the verse below, in which the ford of the Donogue is mentioned, from a man named Pádraig de Bláca, since emigrated to America, but whom I met in the island of Achill. I suppose that fáir must be a participle with ag understood, but I have also heard the line run muna dtagaiḋ tu agus fáir orm. The form tagann for tigeann is very common everywhere. Line 8, for amáin *read* aṁáin.

Page 58, line 12, for ceile *read* céile. Line 25. A northern correspondent has informed me that curaicín means, in parts of Ulster, a comb for the hair, and that this must be the meaning of curaċán here. This would make good sense, but I have never heard the word. The co-operation of everyone is obviously needed, not only to preserve, but also to explain our folk literature. Line 31, ceileaḃair must be meant for ceileaḃraċ "warbling;" however, I give the word as I heard it.

Page 60, line 8. The real form of this play on words is as follows, according to my friend O Ruaiḋriġ's account; "Tumaus was said to have married after Una's death into the O'Rorke family, but was given to the reprehensible habit of stealing off from Castlemore (query, Edmondstown) to visit poor Una's grave in Loch Cé, and was finally found dead upon it one morning—which looks like a bardic touch. It was on the occasion of his marriage, when his father-in-law showed him the fortune in sheep, etc., he said, b'ḟearr liom-sa caora agus

aon uan amháin (=Aon Una Bán) 'ná an méad sin.* "The Shanachies" adds O Ruaidhrigh, "used to lay stress on the fact that O'Rorke, by giving Tumaus a certain amount of sheep and cattle, they, when added to his own stock, would entitle him (Tumaus) to a certain rank of chieftaincy, for which they had an Irish name which I forget; it wasn't *ridiré*. There was an ordinance in the Brehon code of this nature, and it makes me think Tumaus lived at an earlier age than we usually thought." Séaghan O Ruaidhrigh has also furnished me with the following note: "*Dualtach Caoch*, according to some, was his brother and successor, but others said nothing of their relationship except that he was the last chief, and their story of his death was much the same as that given by Prendergast in his "Irish Rapparees," except that the latter makes no mention of Ruane and the clamp of turf, which, of course, was always our version. Prendergast calls him *Sir* Dudley Costello, and says he was killed by a party led by one of the Dillons somewhere beyond Swinford. He had been a Colonel in the service of Charles II., and had served abroad. The place where Ruane is said to have shot him is a hill near Swinford, called to this day *Sithestin a' Dualtaigh*, or, in English, Seeshtheen. Did poor Shamus O'Hart not mention anything of the boyish Tumaus when asked would he try a fall with the champion, "I would if I got enough to eat," "an íosfá an capall sin?" "ní'l fios agam an íosfainn an capall mór acht d'íosfainn an capall beag," † meaning the foal, and the story of the twenty grouse which he and the wrestler demolished, and which was the cause of MacDermott's prejudice against him afterwards in the love affair."

According to the best story-tellers, Tumaus lived at Castlemore, about half-a-mile west of Ballaghaderreen (Bealach a'doirín), in the Co. Mayo, and Una was the daughter of MacDermott of the Rock, who lived in a castle on an island in Loch Cé, called teach na carraige, or the "house of the rock," from whence sprang the present name, Rockingham. Hence the local proverb, d'fhágfainn teach na carraige agad, "I'd leave you the House of the rock," said to an unpleasant companion. Line 26, breáchta is a not uncommon superlative of breágh.

---

* *i.e.* "I'd rather have a single lamb than all that," but the words also mean, "I would rather have one sheep and Fair-haired Una than all that."

† *i.e.* "Would you eat that horse?" "I don't know would I eat the big horse, but I'd eat the little horse." These legends about Tumaus Loidher seem to me an excellent example of how mythic and fabulous elements, the stock-in-trade of storytellers in all ages, become gradually grafted on to a real historical character.

Page 66, line 3. ní ċiúbrainn is the usual form. The people in mid-Connacht never say ní ḃéarfainn; in the last verse of the Coolun, on p. 70, we find the *inverse solecism*, do ṫaḃarfainn for do ḃéarfainn.

Page 69, line 10. *Read* filiḋeaċt for filiḋe aċt. *Read* fuadaċ for fuadac in fourth line of song. Bearnaḋa, in line 6, is often pronounced bearnaċa, and this ċ sound of ḋ in plurals so formed is usual in Connacht. Seáġan O Ruaiḋriġ tells me he is almost certain that it was a man called Curneen who made this song, early in the century, and that the hero of it was one McLachlan, from Airteach, to the west of Castlerea, who carried off a girl from somewhere near Kilmovee, and that the song began Tá bean ag an teampoll a's díolann sí lionn. Curneen was a regular *sporteen* and follower of the gentry, and was the author, according to O Ruaiḋriġ, of many sporting, foxhunting, and drinking songs, but I have been unable to recover any of them.

Page 70. The song of the Coolun is generally associated with Belanagare, in Roscommon, from the first verse, which usually runs, I mbeul-áṫ-na-gcarr atá an stáid-bean ḃreáġ ṁódaṁail; but my inquiries on the spot have elicited nothing to throw light upon it, nor does the song seem well known in the vicinity, so I fancy it must have originated in some other place of the same name.

Page 72, line 7. This line is mistranslated. It does not mean you squeezed a pressure on my hand, but "you pressed an embrace upon me." Barróg is the common form of this word. See p. 48, four lines from bottom, where it is used in its most usual sense.

Page 74, line 14. Táir=tá tu. Line 23. Ní buaileaḋ orm é—I do not well understand this.

Page 76, line 7. Or, perhaps, it should be translated, "what the dead cat," as one would say, "what the mischief." This is how O Ruaiḋriġ explains it. First line of last verse.—O Ruaiḋriġ translates this line differently from me. "In our (Mayo) vernacular," he says, "this would mean 'you passed me by late in the evening without speaking!'" Dorċa was a localism for "cold," "distant," "making strange;" its opposite was suḃáilceaċ. Even in English, "She's as black as the pot" would be heard of a cold, reserved girl without any reference to her complexion."

Page 82. This verse a ṁáire, etc., is, I find, also given by Hardiman,

Page 85, line 1. The mangaire súgaċ (pronounced like Mong-ir-ya Sooguch) means "jovial peddlar," or, something analogous.

Page 86, line 28, *aliter*, dá ndeunfainn caisleán de ċró, *i.e.* if I

were to make a castle of a pigsty. I omitted a seventh verse in the text, which I recovered in the Co. Mayo :—

Ní'l aon ċrann ann san gcoill
    Naċ dtionntóċaḋ a ḃonn os a ḃárr
Ní'l aon eala ar tonn
    Naċ ḋtionntóċaḋ a cúl leis an tsnáṁ
Ná aon tsagart 'san ḃFrainc
    Naċ dtug cúl do aifrionn do ráḋ
Aċt iad ag feiṫeaṁ gaċ am
    Ar ṗéarla deas an tSléiḃ' Ḃáin.

Page 92. This song is supposed to be of Leitrim origin, and is said to be an especial favourite with people of that county. It is, however, well known in Munster also.

Page 94, line 20. *Read* h-aimsiriḋe for hiṁsiriḋe.

Page 98, line 12. *Read* Buḋ for Ruḋ.

Page 100, last line. móinte seems an irregular genitive of móin instead of the usual móna, unless it is for móinteaḋ, the gen. plur., which would not make good sense.

Page 102, line 6. Lasann is very corrupt; it is meant for the relative Lasas=" which lights up." Before this relative form of the verb a " which " (in imitation, according to Dr. Atkinson, of the English "which ") has often been placed of late years.

Page 104, line 1, for aitreaċ *read* aiṫreaċ.

Page 106, line 9. I do not quite know what broḃ is. I have met he expression, broḃ craoiḃe, as well as broḃ luaċra ; it may be the eard of the rush. They have a proverb in Kerry, bailiġeann brob beart which, I suppose, is equivalent to the Scotch " many a little makes a mickle." Is this the same brob with the final b unaspirated ?

Page 114, line 5. *Read* ċruinniuġaḋ for ċruinninġaḋ.

Page 120, line 23. Dún gceannaing cannot be the northern Dungannon, but a place in Waterford of nearly the same name.

Page 122. The first line of this celebrated song ought to run Ṗósfainn Ḃriġdín Ḃeusaiḋ, which is the way I have always heard it, and Mr. John Fleming also, but the manuscript from which I copied wrote ḃeusaċ. O Ruaiḋriġ, who picked up the song by ear, thought that Ḃéusaiḋ was the girl's name " Vesey," but I think beusaiḋ is only another form of beusaċ "well-mannered." My friend, Michael Cavanagh, of Washington, U.S.A. (author of the " Life of Thomas Francis Meagher," and like John O'Mahony, whose private secretary

he once was, a fine Irish scholar), has told me that an old man named John Moloney repeated this song for him from beginning to end, including the bombastic verses stuffed with classical names which I have omitted, and assured him that the celebrated poet, Anthony Raftery, was the author of it, and that it was from Raftery's own lips he heard it. Martin P. Ward, of San Francisco, U.S.A., has also assured me that the piece is Raftery's, and added, that it was made by him one night that he came to the Priest's house in Loughrea, and found a new servant girl before him who did not know him, and was unaware that the priest had given orders that as often as he called he should have a bed and entertainment while he chose to remain. He asked where the other girl, Brígid na Ċaṫasaiġ (Bridget Casey) was, and heard she had gone to the Protestant Minister's house at the other end of the town. It was then he made this poem on her disappearance calling the Minister Pluto, which explains the allusion in the verse, 'Sé Pluto an prionnsa clampraċ sgiob uaim mo stór a's m'annsaċt, etc. Mr. Ward also explains the name Móin-eile which had puzzled me, but which, he says, is the spoken pronunciation of Móin-ailḃe, the Bog of Allen. This piece is not, however, in the only collected manuscript of Raftery's poems which I have seen. A very mutilated edition of it appeared in an Irish-American newspaper some fourteen years ago, the refined and sensitive Gaelic editor omitting nearly every third line as being, he said, "too *broad* and coarse to be submitted to the ladies and gentlemen who compose the (Irish) classes !"—A curious instance of false delicacy.

Page 128, line 22. The true reading of this line is níl mé mór le Charon, and so John Fleming told me he heard it recited, *i.e.* "I am not great with Charon," meaning, according to one of the commonest of Irish idioms—the despair of the merely book-learned—"I am not on good terms with him."

Page 129, note. Mr. H. S. Lloyd who has collected many Ulster and Leinster songs, tells me there is another Bréuch-mhuigh (or Breaky) in Meath, and thinks it is to it the song alludes.

Page 130, line 14. Beir i gcás is an obscure expression to me. I think i gcás must mean, as Tomás O Flannaoile once suggested to me "in trouble," and the line would mean "who would when in trouble give her knowledge of his secret." Cás does often mean "trouble," or "hardship." Line 29. I do not quite understand the meaning of slioċt ġeal saor.

Page 140, line 11. I do not quite understand saor ar ṁéid, nor

the words, dá n-iaḃann tiúin in the next verse. *Read* i bPortláirge in the last verse. Line 13, *read* píob for píoḃ.

Page 142, line 12. Ait which means pleasant in some places, means "queer" in mid-Connacht, just as greannaṁail, which means pleasant in Connacht signifies " queer " in Cork. Can there be a psychological truth underlying this ? Line 22. I think coṁroinn is only the dat. case of cóṁra, a coffin, which reading I have since found in a Meath MS. lent me by my friend, Mr. David Comyn. Line 31, *read* sgríoḃtar for sgrioḃtar.

Page 144, line 5, *read* bréid for ḃréid.

Page 146, line 4, *read* níor for níos. Line 22, *read* ḃíos for bíos. Mr. Comyn's copy, made by one Peadar O Gealacan, near Moynalty, in the Co. Meath, about sixty years ago, prefixes the four following verses to this poem, which I have not met in any of the other copies. I reproduce Peadar's orthography exactly.

Is mairg a ṫaoḃṫaḋ bean mo ḋiaiġ
Fá ċían sin 's a ċiall naċ gar,*
Ní gnáṫ tuile gan trága
Is ionann sin is gráḋ na mban.

Le na ngráḋ na bíoḋ do spéis
Is briseaċ a méin 's as olc a rún
Gráḋ na mban ċugad is uait
Ṫig na ruaig is ṫéid air ccúl.

An t'aon ġráḋ is mó faoi an ngréin
'S a ḃeiṫ aig do ṁnaoi féin ort,
Na creid sin aċ a ḃeiṫ na ḃréig,
'S a ḋol a ḋ éag mur a ṫéid a sop.

Da siúḃalfainn cnoic agus poirt
Do ġeaḃainn a nolc os áird
A Ríġ do ḃeir síneaḋ san ġréin
Go seaċnaiḋ tu mé air a cceárd.

In this copy too, the wife is made to say :

Ní ḃfuigfinn go ḃfuiġinn-se bás
Bruaċ d'uaiṁe, do ráḋ an ḃean,
S ní ḃéinn gan ġruaim air mo ġnaoi
No go ccuirfinn mo ṫaoḃ le d' ċneas.

* I do not quite understand this line.

Accordingly, when the Earl asks her why he was put naked in the tomb, she first says it was done to leave more space for herself to be beside him.

Do ċum uaigneas d'ḟáġail dam féin
Ann sa ccill a ḃfad o ċáċ,
Ċum do aonta, rún mo ċléiḃ
Is fíor a méid-se táim a ráḋ !

Her second excuse is that in the text.

CRÍOCH.